A Life Gone Awry: My Story of the Elan School

By Wayne Kernochan

A LIFE GONE AWRY:
MY STORY OF THE ÉLAN SCHOOL

by Wayne Kernochan

"The tales of treatment at the school during the 1970s were well-documented during the 2002 murder trial of former student Michael Skakel, and the practices of isolating students, screaming sessions called "general meetings" and physically rough treatment have been written about by dozens of former students, including disturbing details of Wayne Kernochan's time at the school between 1978 and 1980 detailed in his e-book, "A Life Gone Awry: My Story of the Elan School."~The Lewiston Sun Journal

SURVIVOR QUOTES ON ELAN SCHOOL

"Former student Matt Hoffman, who boarded at Elan between 1974 and 1976, had nothing good to say about the program Wednesday, calling the campus a "sadistic, brutal, violent, soul-eating hellhole." Lewiston Sun Journal, March 24th, 2011

"This story brought up old hurts, wounds and anger. I was a resident at Elan for almost 2 years, I watched Elan change into a violent atmosphere in a matter of years. I witnessed the change in residents being brought to Elan from Mental facilities, Juvenile detention centers, Autistic children ect....I watched Staff and Directors leave en-mass and I watched 3 people who are still there deny they are doing children harm, It is beyond shameful." ~Danny Bennison in a post on Fornits.com

SURVIVOR COMMENTS ON A LIFE GONE AWRY: MY STORY OF THE ELAN SCHOOL

"I can't thank you enough for telling your story. I have felt alone for many years and because of your story now I don't"~ Debi Levin Johnson

"Wayne's book about elan , lucid , vivid , captures the grist and grinding of what it was like to be in elan , even during my time which was 7-74 to 7-76.(a couple of years before Wayne). This book touches me to my very being. It cuts thru to the marrow in my bones." Matt Hoffman

REGARDING SOCIAL MEDIA FEEDBACK

"By e-mail and private message I've been asked what my family thinks of this....I hadn't considered that before. I don't blame them for sending me to Elan--they didn't know.

It's probably hard to read if ya love someone, but I think the benefit is that they see how easily parents are fooled.

I don't remember anyone blaming their parents while I was there come to think of it."~Wayne Kernochan

A LIFE GONE AWRY:
My Story Of The Elan School

By Wayne Kernochan

Chapter One

An early frost killed the fall colors that year. Everything died before becoming beautiful. The Great Blizzard of 1978 had come and gone, leaving Connecticut buried in snow and its residents in the mire of an ugly winter.

When the call came the night before, informing my parents that I had been accepted at Élan School in Poland Springs, Maine, the man on the phone said I should come right away. I wanted my father to drive because there was snow in the forecast, but the man said the school would fly me the next morning in their private jet.

There were two things on my mind as we climbed the stairs to the glass doors leading into Danbury airport: Airplane crashes and Roy Sullivan. In the past, year jumbo jets had fallen from the sky like four-hundred-ton snowflakes. There had been crashes in Guatemala, Havana and Bombay, and in Tenerife, two Boeing 747 jets collided on the ground killing 583 people. Those places weren't very close to home, but in December a Douglas DC-3 crashed, killing the University of Evansville basketball team, and in October three members of the rock group, Lynyrd Skynyrd, were killed as they attempted an emergency landing in Gillsburg Mississippi.

I called Doctor Peck and told him about my fear of flying, but he explained to me the amazing odds against being in a plane crash, and told me it was safer to fly than drive, but I thought of Roy Sullivan, a park ranger in Virginia who had just been hit by lightning for the seventh time. My father looked at me when we heard about it on the TV set. "Sounds like something that would happen to you," he said.

Bad luck and bad timing were my forte. If there was a wrong turn to take or a wrong time to do something, I would find it. As the insanity in my head became worse, so did my luck. I was convinced that I was going to die in a plane crash.

The wind blew; causing Mom to duck her head. I lost my balance and my hat almost blew off, so I grabbed the hat with one hand and handrail with the other, steadying myself on the wet stairs. "Wow, I almost fell. The wind…"

Mom pulled the door open. "C'mon," she said. "Damn the wind."

#

Danbury airport was the size of a supermarket, not what I expected for a major traffic hub. Even the planes were small. In New York City we took commercial jets, and though bigger planes crashed, everyone died on impact. Small planes always went down in icy waters, rarely killing everyone onboard, leaving survivors to suffer before they die.

Mom looked tired. Her clothes didn't fit, and her hair was undone, which was unusual for her. She was anxious, and rushed me the whole morning, as if she wanted the trip to be over. She was intense and silent the whole day. There were seven other kids at home to take care of and the stress was taking its toll on her. I could see that she felt bad about my leaving, but I could also see that she felt guilty for being relieved that I was going.

As she dealt with the woman at the desk, I pointed to the vending machines. "I'm gonna go get a Coke."

She paused the conversation with a hand gesture. "Get me one, would you?"

"You got it."

In spite of a snow warning the woman at the desk said I was going to fly to Lewiston Airport. I didn't understand the extreme urgency but was happy to be getting away from home. I needed a break from my family as much as they needed one from me, so when Doctor Peck suggested Élan, I was happy to go—I just wanted to drive.

I considered the coffee machine for a second, but my stomach told me not to. I got two cans of Coke and returned to the desk. "Here ya go."

"Thanks."

#

To Mom, for one day, on March 23rd, 1963, I was the miracle child because I wasn't supposed to be born alive. The umbilical cord had broken the day she went to the hospital, so, they did an emergency cesarean section, and I was born into the world in horror. I didn't remember it, but Doctor Peck told me that my subconscious did, which affected me nonetheless.

That may have been the reason for the nightmares. I had them for as long as I could remember, but they got worse at ten years of age and I went from miracle child to problem child. I wet the bed until I was a teenager, and dreamed of monsters. I said the wrong thing at the wrong time and got into trouble at school and play. I stole money from my parents and fought with my siblings.

By the age of twelve the monsters in my sleep began to haunt me when I was awake. Though I knew they weren't real, I saw bloody, violent flashes, which scared me, so I said or did inappropriate things to get away from people. At thirteen years old I was caught lighting fires by a neighbor, and my parents realized my behavior was more than just growing pains.

The guidance counselors, psychologists and psychiatrists were a waste of time because I lied to them all. They reported to my parents, and my parents made fun of our Uncle Mike for being crazy. I didn't want them to humiliate me that way. They called him Mike Loose because he was loose in the head, and my brothers laughed.

My brothers already made fun of me. They called my bedroom Wayne's Pissaria so I let the shrinks believe that I was acting out for my parent's attention. My father beat me with hockey sticks: his attention was the last thing I wanted. But, it was better they believe that than know the truth.

My psychologist, Doctor Adler, suggested Vitam, a drug program in Norwalk, Connecticut, and though I hadn't done drugs, I wanted to get away from home. I did better there, and my family seemed to do better without me, so the relief was mutual. After Vitam it was clear that a drug program wasn't going to help me, so that was a concern when Élan was suggested.

"I liked Vitam," I told Doctor Peck, "but, I didn't have anything in common with the people there…they were all drug addicts."

"Vitam was a mistake," Doctor Peck said. "Élan is different."

"Really?"

"Élan specializes in troubled adolescents, and has a ninety-five percent success rate," he said. "It's like school, with therapy. They have counselors and psychiatrists, and activities."

He was very convincing.

\#

The pilot looked like a pilot, with his official hat and jacket. He was old and sure of himself, so I relaxed a bit. He spoke to Mom first. "Hi, I'm Jim," he said, and shook her hand. "I'm going to do this run."

He shook my hand next. He had hairy hands, like the monster in my dreams. "I hope the plane don't crash," I said.

Everyone stopped and stared at me. I regretted saying it as soon as I did, and was as shocked by what I said as they were. It was a line from a Bill Cosby comedy routine, so I knew why it was in my head, but something told me that it was inappropriate, and not to say it, and my mind agreed, but my mouth said it anyway.

"Wayne!" Mom said.

"I'm sorry." I hung my head.

"Don't worry about it," Jim said. "It was a joke."

Mom turned to me. "So, I guess this is goodbye."

As happy as I was to be leaving, I wasn't. "I guess."

"I'll come up and visit as soon as I can."

"Okay."

I turned and gestured for Jim to lead the way. We started towards the tall grey doors to our left. I didn't look back.

\#

We passed through the doors, went down a hallway, which led to another door, which let us out to the runway. There, a six-passenger twin-engine plane sat with its engines running. "Get in the front seat," he said. "I need you there to take off."

"Do you?"

"I can't take off or land without a copilot."

He was being nice, I knew, because he would then have no way of getting back, but I smiled and climbed into the front seat like a starry eyed kid. "Cool."

Jim taxied us to the runway, cleared us for takeoff and took to the air. My stomach felt queasy on the way up, but when we leveled off it passed. I looked out at the ground below to check for icy waters.

\#

The airport in Maine was smaller than the one we left. It was simple and quiet, and there were only two runways. They were expecting us, obviously, because there was a group of people there to greet us—two men in work uniforms, a man in a suit and a mid-twenties hippie-looking guy in jeans and a ski parka.

The two workmen didn't mind me as I got out, but the man in the suit greeted me, and introduced me to Mark. I shook his hand. "Good to meet you."

"Same here."

When we had my things, Mark and I got into a striped Chevy van, and started down the road. "You don't have any drugs on you, do you?"

I shook my head. "I've never done drugs."

"Oh, so you're court ordered."

"No, I've never been arrested."

He laughed. "Then what are you doing here?"

I shrugged. "I'm a problem kid."

"Well, if you don't cause any problems for a while, you'll be going home in a year to eighteen months," he said. "Some people go through the program in less than a year."

"How long can you stay if you like it?" I asked.

He laughed again and turned down a road that looked like it went nowhere. We drove quietly for a while as if he didn't want to burst my bubble by telling me that I wasn't going to summer camp. Eventually he pulled into a clearing and said, "Here we are."

It looked like a camp, with small cabins and a bigger, more administrative looking house. Mark pulled up next to the bigger one. That's when I heard the screaming. It started out as one voice, was followed by another, and then another.

Mark led me toward the screams, unbothered. "It's not all that bad, Wayne. You'll get used to it soon."

"What's all that yelling?"

"That," he said, "is a haircut."

"What's a haircut?"

"If you do something wrong you get yelled at. Sometimes there are three or four people who do it. It's called a haircut."

Only the staff did that at Vitam, and they didn't scream with the venom these people did. I knew there would be discipline, but this was bad. I already wanted to go home.

What greeted us entering the main house was something out of

11

Alice in Wonderland. People were dressed up like babies and Klansmen, and people with signs and household appliances hanging around their necks wandered the huge house as others shouted at them angrily, berating and degrading them. There were people with cups and plates strung around their necks like chunky junky jewelry. Everyone was screaming at everyone else.

The Klansmen were actually dunces, wearing dunce caps and signs that explained why. My Vitam experience told me that these were punishments, and that Élan was going to be more than simple discipline, so I told Mark that I wanted to go home.

"You don't get to go home."

"What do you mean I don't get to go home?" I said. "I'm not mandated here. I was told that if I didn't like it I could leave."

"Then you were lied to, Wayne. You're not going home for a while."

He was telling the truth. Doctor Peck and my family had lied to get rid of me.

#

I spent the first night in the dorm of Élan Three because it was late. Though I was going to be a resident of Élan Seven, they kept me in Three to go over the rules, and do what they called 'pulling you into the program'.

Mark told me that I had to sing at the morning meeting, in front of fifty people. "I can't sing in front of all these people," I said.

"You have to."

I was angry for being abandoned and deceived. "I'm not doing it."

"You will, though. Everyone does it."

"Not me."

#

When I repeated this during the morning meeting, I was allowed to sit back down. It wasn't without warning. "You'll sing down at your house," Peter McCann said, "and you'll dance as well."

"No, I won't."

He laughed.

#

I was sent down the hill to Élan Seven a few hours later. The house at the bottom of the hill had the same yelling coming from it that Élan Three had, but by that time I was used to it. I understood that Élan was just a super-strict version of Vitam, and to get along I was going to have to play ball.

The first thing I noticed about Élan Seven was that there were black and Hispanic people there. Three was only white kids, so I asked Stan, the guy Mark turned me over to, why. "Three is for rich kids. We're the lower class here because we're from the streets."

"Why am I here then?"

"I don't know. But you can ask Danny Bennison when you talk to him."

"Who's Danny Bennison?"

"Danny runs the house. All new residents speak to the director in the first few days."

"Good. Maybe he'll let me out of here."

#

I was introduced to Danny Bennison a few hours later when the house was ushered into the dining room, as if for a fire drill. The older residents, who patrolled the house with clipboards and did security—what Stan called 'Expeditors'—came out of their office screaming at the top of their lungs. "General meeting!"

We were ordered to sit in the dining room in silence with our hands folded on the table, to wait for whatever was coming. The quiet was harder on the senses than the constant commotion. Finally, my director came out and I knew it was going to be bad. He had a white mesh laundry bag with bright red boxing gloves in it, and everyone froze when they saw it.

He threw the bag against the wall, and there was a thud. Then he looked at the waiting crowd and at Mike Calabrese in particular. "Get the fuck up here."

Mike was dressed like a baby, with a bonnet and diaper. He wore a sign that he read every time he entered or left a room. He shook his rattle first. "Waa, Waa, Waa. I'm Mike Calabrese, and I'm a big baby. Please confront me about why I act out and make everyone miserable if I don't get my way. Waa, Waa, Waa."

Mike didn't move fast enough, so Danny grabbed him by the neck and dragged him in front of the room. "I said get the fuck up there!" he yelled, and threw Mike against the wall.

Danny was physically imposing, with a smug face and perfectly feathered hair. He was a dark-haired moustache-and-attitude badass-white guy, and he was good at it. I was afraid of him immediately.

"What the fuck is your problem, Mike Calabrese? I have a pile of incident reports in my office, and your fucking name is on every one of them."

Mike said nothing.

"I asked you a fucking question!"

"I don't have a problem."

Danny turned to the house, and said calmly, "Would you people like to tell him his problem?"

Suddenly, everyone jumped up from their seats and rushed at Mike. They stood inches away from him, screaming in his face. It was angry and bitter, and they sprayed him with saliva as they yelled. It lasted five minutes. When it was over Mike wiped the spit from his face.

"So, what do you have to say for yourself, Michael?" Danny asked. "You have the fucking audacity to question my expeditor in the kitchen, and then stand here telling me you don't have a problem. I think you have a problem with authority as well as a lot of other things, you big fucking baby."

He broke off and looked at the crowd, "Who wants to go in the ring with this motherfucker?"

Hands went up, and Danny picked the biggest guy in the room to have a boxing match with Mike. Mike resisted putting the gloves on, so, Danny had four guys hold him down while they spanked him with a racquetball paddle. He fought, but was outmatched. The paddle had holes drilled in it to maximize the pain. When he shouted out, I turned away: and looked instead at Danny Bennison, who was smiling. "Are you going to put the gloves on now Mike?"

They tried again, and Mike fought again. He was thrown back down and paddled some more. "Ten…ten more…Next… Ten…ten more…Next…" As good a fight as Mike fought, I could see that he was going to lose. It was brutal to watch.

When Mike put on the boxing gloves, guys from the house who were physically superior to him beat him into submission. I kept waiting to hear what he did to deserve such battering and humiliation, but all I heard was that it was 'for being a baby'.

As the general meeting went on, Danny told the house about his prison experiences. "You're going to prison someday, Michael," he said. Then he looked at the rest of us. "All of you people are going to end up in prison with attitudes like this."

He shifted back to Mike. "You, they'll just gang rape in the shower, you fat piece of shit." Then he held everyone's attention as he described sitting in his cell listening to a young man being raped. "I sat on the end of my bed wondering when they were going to come for me," he warned.

#

I ran to catch up with Stan after the general meeting was over. "What was that?" I asked.

"That was a general meeting..."

I cut him off. "I know what a general meeting is, Stan. I told you that I know certain things from being in Vitam. I mean the boxing ring and the paddle. What's the deal with that?"

"They have a physical abuse license. If someone is physically violent, they can punish him with the ring or spankings."

I didn't say a word, but he knew what I was thinking. "Wayne, if you just do what you gotta do, and keep your nose clean, you don't have to go through any of that."

I sang and danced the next morning without a fight.

Chapter Two

The yelling was constant, and there was no way to stop it. If you were going fast enough for their liking, they found something else to yell at you about. It would have been pointless if it wasn't a prelude to the boxing ring or paddle. I did as I was told, and stood silent when they gave me my first haircut.

Though I was there for four hours—and two of those were in a general meeting—they decided that I wasn't sharing enough about my feelings. It made no sense, but I thought about Mike Calabrese's face when they beat him, and stayed quiet. I also remembered Danny's advice to the house about injustices before the G.M. broke up.

"If you don't like something around here, and you think it's unfair...rub it on your chest." That didn't really make sense either, but his message was clear. "Shut up, and do as you're told."

After lunch, Stan took me to his office, and said "You'll be starting off where everyone else does...on the service crew." He pointed to a chalkboard, with the job positions written on it. "I'm your boss, or department head, and George Rees is my boss, your coordinator."

He introduced me to my peers, Gary Ross, Jane Tolar, and Lisa Groton. "You guys will stick together most of the time because you're all new."

My three peers helped Stan acquaint me with the routine. In the morning, we cleaned the house, and as we did that the coordinators gave haircuts to the people in their crew. At noon we had lunch, cleaned up some more, and had groups until dinner. "After dinner, we clean some more," Stan said, "and then we have school, and free-time."

"Unless you have no privileges," Gary Ross said. "Then you clean some more."

"After snack, we clean up again, then we carry the cleaning equipment to the dorms when we go to bed at night," Stan said.

"It's a lot of work, but you'll get used to it."

"And, then there are the rules..." Yvette Portella cut in. "Let's not forget the rules."

Yvette was an expeditor, and they were in charge of the security in the house. There were five expeditors, and their boss was Dave Winston, who spent most of his time with staff. Yvette was there to tell us about the rules, but Stan did most of the talking.

He explained cardinal rules. "No sex, no drugs, and no physical violence," he said, then he told us that the cardinal rules were strictly enforced, but didn't have to. I saw the brand of discipline they used. Gary, Lisa and Jane didn't need to be told either. We knew that if we were caught breaking one of the cardinal rules, we were dead.

"Another thing to know, "Yvette said, "is that new residents are not allowed to hang around together."

"But, Stan told us we have to hang out together," Gary said.

Yvette smirked. "Wise guy, huh?"

"You can be together as long as there's an older resident with you," Stan said. "It's just that we don't want you sneaking off together."

"And another big one is splitting," Yvette said. "If you take off, you get killed."

"I'm surprised anyone here is alive," I said.

Yvette punched me in the shoulder playfully. "Yo, don't make me kill you."

We laughed.

#

As we cleaned the dining room Gary Ross told me his story. He had done stick-ups, shot heroin, and driven stolen cars. "I was arrested two days out of Daytop, and they sent me here," he said. "It was either here or Long Lane again."

Daytop was a drug program, like Élan, but they didn't have a license to beat their residents. I had heard about it at Vitam, but hadn't heard of Long Lane.

"What's Long Lane?" I asked.

Gary put down his bucket. "That's right. You've never been arrested, have you?"

"No."

Gary and Lisa took turns telling me about the Long Lane

School. They called it 'The Farm'. "It was a fucking prison for kids," Gary said.

"Gary Ross! Watch your language," Jane said.

"It was."

#

After lunch we had encounter group, which was where we dealt with our anger. If someone pisses you off, you waited your turn. When one person was done screaming at someone, you proceed to scream at the person you want to scream at. That person usually begins screaming at you until you're both done, at which time someone else begins screaming at you, that person, or someone else. If no one screams at anyone else fast enough you can begin screaming at someone else altogether. It was loud.

The banter was vicious. You weren't allowed to threaten anyone, so instead; they said what they would like to do to each other. You couldn't say 'I'll break your fucking legs' but you could say 'I'd like to break your fucking legs' or 'if we were out there, I'd break your fucking legs'. Anything 'out there' was allowed; it's hypothetical. 'Suck my dick' was out but 'if we were out there, I'd have you sucking my dick' was fine. The context was clear. The people in Élan Seven were angry and wanted to hurt each other.

Gary Ross started the group off by going after Jane Tolar for being a slut. Jane went back at him for a lewd remark he made in the kitchen.

"Fuck you, you whore…"

"Fuck you, you piece of shit …"

"You said to me in the dining room …"

"When we were in the dining room…"

"I'd like to…"

"If we were out there…"

And on it went.

#

When attacked, I become numb or defensive. Defensiveness was reserved for threats, so I got numb when Gary turned on me because it wasn't one. He was 'pulling me up' about the fact that I didn't share my feelings. I didn't say a word until he was done.

"I have nothing to say," I said, "because I have nothing in common with you people."

Donald's eyes widened at the term 'you people', so I beat him to the punch. "I don't mean 'you people', I mean all of you people…I've never done drugs, and that's all you guys talk about."

"You earned your seat here," Donald said, "one way or another."

"But I've never done drugs, and that's all you guys ever talk about. I have nothing to say."

"You've never even tried them?" Jane asked.

"Never."

"Then what are you doing here?"

"I keep asking the same question."

Donald pointed out that Élan was for more than just drugs, and told us that lots of people had graduated without ever having done them. He didn't sound convinced of what he was saying. "Talk to Danny about this," he said.

\#

The second half of encounter group was for resolving the problems of the people that confronted each other in the first half. The person who got the worst of it was up to the staff member running the group. Being ex-junkies, they were good manipulators, and pinned the blame on the person they didn't like.

Gary got the worst of it with Jane. It was obvious that he was attracted to her, but Donald went past that to 'reverse racism', which got my attention. Donald wasn't very intelligent, so he acted like a street-tough sophisticate, but he didn't hide his lack of education well.

"What's reverse racism?" I asked.

"It's when black people hate white people," he said.

"Wouldn't that just be racism?"

"What do you mean?"

"Wouldn't the reverse of racism be non-racism?"

Donald looked one-upped for a second, and then said, "You know what the hell I mean." He continued questioning Gary Ross, blamed him for the incident in the kitchen, and didn't argue the accusation about Jane being a slut. Danny deemed her a slut, and that's all there was to it. We weren't allowed to disrespect Danny's decisions behind his back.

Denise McDaniel was the senior resident in the group, and didn't like Gary Ross, so she helped Donald tear him to shreds.

19

When they were done with Gary, the rest of the group was amateur pop-psychology meted-out by Donald and Denise, like bologna sandwiches at the county jail; it was cold and tasteless, and did little good. I smoked cigarettes and spaced out for the rest of the group.

#

That night, after school, the expeditors came out of Danny's office, shouting 'General Meeting'. We gathered in the dining room, sat in silence with our hands folded, everyone hoping that whatever it was didn't include them. I hadn't done anything, and yet I was afraid. That fear increased when Danny kicked the door open and threw the bag of boxing gloves out ahead of him.

Debbie Dole had mouthed off to Donald earlier, so she stood up and walked to the front of the room without being called. Danny laughed. "You bet your ass this is about you, ya titless bitch. Who the fuck do you think you are?"

She slowed down to answer the question, but Danny grabbed her and threw her against the wall. She hit it as hard as Mike Calabrese had that morning and when she did, I knew we were in the hands of a sociopath. Danny Bennison liked to hurt people.

Donald Hampton was a new staff member. The story Gary Ross told me was that he beat a man to death in the adult corrections center in Rhode Island. He was broad and muscular, and had crazy eyes, plus, he went through Parsonsfield, the lockup unit, so I was convinced the story was true.

Danny said to Debbie, "Do you think that because you're going home, you can talk to my staff any way you want?"

Debbie was in reentry, which was the final stage of Élan, so she was on her way out the door. Stan told me that reentry people rarely participated in house events and were allowed out to bars to drink. Until the beginning of the meeting I had no idea they got the same discipline we did.

Debbie shrugged. "I…"

Danny cut her off, looked at the room, and said, "Who has something they want to say to this bitch?"

The older residents rushed to the front of the dining room and screamed obscenities at Danny's command. I stayed in my seat, afraid to get up. Finally, the crowd finished and Debbie wiped the spit from her face.

20

"So what do you have to say for yourself?" Danny said. "Do you think you can go out there in the streets with this kind of attitude?" He paused. "You'll be sucking dick for drugs in a week…a day."

"No, I won't."

"Look at you. Ya look like a prostitute…except for those ingrown tits of yours. How did you end up with ingrown tits?" He laughed. "I guess you have to blow guys that like young boys."

Donald laughed at that, and said, "Ya know, we'd shoot you down and keep you longer, but you're hopeless. You've gotten nothing out of being here."

"Oh, there's no way I'm keeping you here," Danny said. "You're a fucking cancer, so next Thursday, you're out."

The degrading remarks about Debbie's tits went on for another half hour, and then, Danny had girls from the house beat on her in the ring the same way the men beat on Mike. When that was over, he had the men spank Debbie with the paddle.

\#

There was one last piece of business when Danny was done with Debbie. He looked at me and said, "Get up."

I did. My knees were weak, so my body shook as I stood at attention.

"So, you want to know why you're here."

"I was told this wasn't a drug program…"

Danny cut me off. "It's not. It's a therapeutic community for emotionally disturbed individuals—of which you are one. You flunked out of the last place you were in, and your parents don't want you back, even when you're done here." He got in my face. "They want us to put you in a foster home."

I looked at the ground.

"Time will answer your questions," Danny said, "and that's all I have to say on the subject at this time."

With that, the subject was closed.

Chapter Three

Niggers—we had 'em. We also had spics, dykes, faggots and bitches. Danny's language was foul and he didn't hide his disdain for any of us. As the general meetings became more so did the list of abuses. I avoided confrontation and thanked God that I was only being yelled at.

Fear factored into every move we made. Even older residents weren't immune to the insanity. In my first week, two people in positions of authority were shot down; they lost their jobs, had their privileges taken away and were sent to scrub floors for minor infractions of the rules.

'Shot downs' wore shorts, signs and costumes, and got the brunt of the one-on-one haircuts for something stupid, like not cleaning fast enough or well enough. When they weren't eating or in school, they worked and did service crew jobs so we hung out with them a lot. I became friends with Mike Calabrese.

Mike had been in Élan for thirteen months and was shot down for most of that time, but he didn't seem broken by it. I liked Mike because he told stories about the old days; when Alan Frey was the director and the house was corrupt.

"Corrupt...Ya mean, worse than this?"I asked.

"Much worse than this," he said. "Alan was a sick fuck."

"Really?"

"There was a sign on the T.V. that said 'If you touch this television without permission, you're dead'."

We weren't allowed to talk about past staff members like that, and Stan was supposed to report us for doing it, but he sat at his desk, smoking a cigarette. When Mike started telling the story of the night George White kidnapped a night guard with a kitchen knife, Stan stopped him. "Let's stop with the war stories, huh?"

Mike laughed, and changed the subject.

\#

At regular group, or what we called 'static group', people

shared about their past. That afternoon Danny was seated in the group leader's chair so I was apprehensive immediately. He showed contempt when he spoke to me at Debbie Dole's G.M. so I was more afraid of him than ever.

"Everybody, sit down, and let's get this started," Danny said. "We don't have a lot of time."

There were eleven of us seated in a circle. Danny told us that we were going to go around the room so that everyone could share for a minute about how they were feeling. I was seventh in line and had nothing to say, but with Danny there I needed to think of something.

Dave went first. "I feel great. I'm doing what I gotta do, and getting closer to going home, every day."

Next, Denise complained about how hard it was being in charge of the expeditors, and then Jane Tolar complained that she was getting tired of losing privileges because of a few people's behavior. Gary said that he was okay, but not feeling well, and Stan talked about falling behind at work, and how he needed to 'dig himself'. Mark Strickland said he missed having privileges. I froze.

"So?" Danny said. "We're waiting."

I was bereft of any feeling but fear, but couldn't talk about that, so I shrugged.

"Well, c'mon," Danny said. "Say something."

"I don't know what to say."

"Oh, Jesus Christ, you're not going to start that 'I don't belong here' shit again, are you?"

"No, I'm just not feeling bad about anything."

"Really," he said. "So everything was okay with your home life?"

"It was bad, but not too bad."

"From what I'm hearing, your daddy was never home, and he ran around with his friends while your mother was taking care of the kids and the house."

Danny sensed that he had me, so he followed my obvious stunned look by telling the group about the night my sister was born, and how my father was drunk at a poker game when he got the call. When my family talked about it, it was as a joke because my father didn't usually drink, but the way Danny told it made my father sound like a drunken degenerate. I was afraid to contradict him, and stayed quiet.

When he was done he looked at Yvette Portella. "So, how are you doing today?" Yvette told us. Robert Gamble and Lisa Groton followed. Danny finished with Wayne Weaver. "So, how are you adjusting to being an expeditor?"

"Good," Wayne said. "Good."

"Really? Because you look like you have the weight of the world on your shoulders."

Wayne laughed, and lit a Marlboro menthol. "I'm just taking my job too seriously."

Danny followed that with a two minute speech about how he wanted people that were too serious about their job, rather than not serious enough. Wayne didn't nod or smile because though Danny was complimenting him, he wasn't. Wayne could feel that Danny didn't like him, and I could too. It was obvious in the tone of his voice.

Danny picked Robert Gamble to share first. Robert told us that he was doing what he had to do, but Danny disagreed. "I don't hear about what got you here. Why aren't you sharing about that?"

"I don't know."

"Why don't you enlighten the group?"

For the next ten minutes Robert told us his story. He was court ordered to Élan for killing a man. Danny didn't show disdain for Robert. I watched his face as he confronted him, and he seemed to like him. Then he had Robert tell us why he did it.

"Because he was a faggot."

"Did he touch you?"

"No."

"Did he try to?"

"No."

Danny shook his head. "So, you killed the guy, just because he was a freak?"

Robert nodded.

The group stopped because Peter McCann came through the front door. He was followed by a man I didn't recognize. They called Danny over and went into the coordinators office. A few minutes later Dave was called in, and a minute after, he came out and yelled "General meeting."

#

There isn't a good answer to the question 'Why are you staring at my tits?' but with Denise McDaniel you better damn well come up with one. I didn't get the confrontation from her because I wouldn't let he catch me staring, even though her tits were her best asset. She got too much of a thrill from degrading guys she did catch.

Denise gave particular attention to Gary Ross when she was in charge, and caught him staring when we stopped in front of Élan Three's porch. It was warm, and Denise's top was very revealing. "I'm not looking at your chest," Gary said.

"Yes you did, Gary Ross. Now, dig yourself, and get in line."

"If I was staring at your chest," Gary said, "I would've fell asleep."

"Gary Ross, just get in line, Stupid!"

We weren't allowed to call each other names or yell at each other outside group unless it was after asking someone to do something more than twice. The third time, you were allowed to call them stupid, and you were allowed to yell it. They called it a 'pull up', which was supposed to be reserved for extreme disrespect, but like the yelling it was overdone and rarely effective. When it had any effect, it exacerbated a bad situation.

"Gary Ross, knock on that tree," Robert Gamble said.

Usually a haircut was given inside, behind closed doors, but in slim times there were exceptions. They could give one anywhere and make you knock on anything, so Gary knocked on the tree like he was knocking on a door.

"Who's out there?"

"Gary."

"Come in!"

Gary took a step forward like he was entering a room, and Robert screamed at him for disrespecting Denise, causing a commotion in line, and making us look bad in front of another house. The guys on Élan Three's front porch were watching the whole time.

When Robert was done, Gary got back in line, silent. "Does anybody have anything else to say before they make us look bad in front of Élan Three?" Denise said. "Because I'm tired of always looking like the street house."

\#

Inside Élan Three's dining room there were chairs lined up in rows, and expeditors from each house steered their people where they were supposed to sit. It was quiet considering how many people were in the room. We, from Élan Seven, were placed in the back. It was easy to spot our house because Three and Five had all white people.

Parsonsfield had niggers, spics, faggots, and bitches too, but we never interacted with them because they were far away. They were a lockup unit for the real bad guys according to what I heard. Waterford wasn't a lockup unit, but it was in a different location as well, so we didn't interact with them either. When Three, Five or Seven needed large numbers of people to scream at and to spit on someone, we did it together because we were close.

When Peter McCann came out, the room quieted a little more. He was big and burley. According to Mike Calabrese, Peter had hands of steel. "When he yelled at me, he poked my chest with his finger. It was like being poked with a pool cue," he said.

The stranger that came into our house with Peter was Marty Kruglick, the director of Élan Five. He stood next to Peter, Danny on his right. Elaine Eisenberg was in the corner, on the stage behind them.

"So, we're here to welcome Elaine back," Peter said. He turned to the two expeditors watching her. "Get her over here."

I met Elaine when I was at Élan Three. She was perky, had a pretty face, and was nicely dressed, but when she stood up I could see she had been through a rough time. Her hair and clothes were disheveled and she was dirty.

The people from Élan Three started to grumble and Peter sensed it, so, he turned to them. "Who wants to welcome Elaine back?"

They didn't wait for her to get off the stage. Everyone rushed up onto it and surrounded her. Residents from my house and Élan Five joined in, but I didn't. Most of us didn't. We were the house at the bottom of the hill, so most of us didn't qualify.

When they were done, Marty took over. "You know what I wanna know?" he said. "I wanna know how the fuck you got all the way to California? How did you pull that off?"

Elaine didn't say anything.

"I asked you a question."

She shrugged. "I hitchhiked."

"You hitchhiked?" Marty said. "Really?"

"Yeah."

"Yeah" He mimicked her.

Peter cut in. "You seriously expect us to believe that you got from Maine to California with your thumb alone?"

Danny laughed at that.

"I don't know what you mean."

Marty laughed. "Bullshit," he said. "Gas, grass or ass, no one rides free. And, you only had your ass with you when you left here."

"Well, I didn't do that."

"C'mon," Marty said. "You didn't suck dick for rides?"

"No."

"Bullshit."

It went on for twenty minutes. Marty did his best to cajole Elaine into admitting that she had sex for rides like a truck stop hooker, but she stuck to her story that people were nice to her. When Peter and Marty knew they weren't going to get her to say what they wanted, they prompted the crowd to charge her once more.

Marty wouldn't let it go. "So, who picked you up?"

"Truck drivers, mostly."

Marty had an evil look in his eyes. I was convinced that Elaine was telling the truth, as were most of the people in the room, but he wanted something and wasn't going to stop until he got it. "So, you expect us to believe that they drove you around out of the kindness of their hearts?"

"Yes."

"You're a fucking liar. Who wants to go in the ring with her?"

For two hours, Elaine stuck to her story as Marty had her spanked with the paddle and yelled at and spit on. The physical abuse was bad, but the filth that came out of Marty's mouth made it worse. He wanted her spirit. He pushed to get something sexual out of Elaine, like he was appeasing a sexual fantasy in public, and when it didn't work he got angry. Eventually, he wore her down and forced her to say that she was raped, and that the man who did it defecated on her when he was done.

The crowd lost some of its vigor when it was clear that she was saying she was raped to stop the abuse, but they deadpanned when he made her say that she was shit on. They were less venomous when they went up to yell, and Marty could sense that he was losing them, so he went on to what costume she would be wearing and what her punishment would be. When it was over none of us spoke about it, which was rare after a general meeting.

\#

School made no sense. We were all lumped into the same grade no matter age or education, for two hours a night. I didn't mind the short day because the less chance of getting in trouble in school, the better. Acting out there was dealt with more severely than normal.

During second period I raised my hand.

"Yes," Mister Dionne said.

"May I use the bathroom?"

"Sure," he said, "but, use the one in the expeditor's office... Miss Russell is using the one in the back."

Miss Russell was my favorite teacher. She had a pretty, freckled face, and a body like a porn star. It was hard to see because she wore conservative clothes, but it was there. She was done, I knew, because I could hear her voice in the class in the living room. I wanted the solitude of a locked door so I went to the bathroom in the back. I realized that it wasn't her voice when I opened the door and she stood there with her blouse open, fixing her brassiere.

"Wayne!"

"I'm sorry."

She covered herself, but it was too late—I had seen it all. Her initial shock wore off, so she looked out the door to see if anyone else had seen. There was no one in the back room, so she looked at me. "Get out of here before someone catches you."

I turned. "I'm sorry," I repeated, and left.

\#

After the filth I heard at Elaine's general meeting, I thought my dick would never get hard again, but Miss Russell cured me. That night, when we were in the dorm, and the lights were out, I thought of her tits and masturbated.

Jerking off was tricky to get away with in a room with four

guys, and though everyone said it was normal, it was treated like a sin, so I needed to be careful. I checked the door, and then looked to my left at Matt Brennan, and stopped.

He smiled, because he was looking at me and doing the same thing, like we were doing it together. He was a fag.

Chapter 4

March was bitter cold and it snowed almost every day, but the worst was the wind. It drove the snow sideways and intensified the cold, making it almost unbearable to be outside. By the middle of the month I was relegated to shoveling the path from the house to the dorm because Danny took an interest in me.

I liked Vitam in spite of the fact that I didn't fit in, because people liked me and didn't treat me like a kid. They included me in things and didn't make fun of me. I could have left anytime I wanted, but didn't. The good times ended when I was introduced to Kip Neville.

Kip was admittedly gay, and confronted the guys about homosexuality in group all the time. I didn't like him because he enjoyed it. He sensed that and did his worst to try and get me to admit that I had homosexual thoughts. I hadn't, but Kip didn't believe me and was deliberately mean to me. In return I deliberately pissed him off until I was thrown out.

The question came up in a group that Danny was running, and if Élan was the therapeutic community Doctor Peck said it was, I might have been willing to share what was really wrong with me, but Danny was never going to hear it. Because of the torture Kip put me through at Vitam, I told the group that I had thoughts but was straight. Danny asked if I had ever had sex with a guy, and I told him that I hadn't, but he said "I don't believe you."

"I don't either," Robert Gamble said. "I see the way you look at me in the shower."

"What are you talking about?" I said. "I never looked at you in the shower."

"Oh, yes you did. I knew you were a faggot the second I laid eyes on you."

"Now you're just being stupid."

Robert asked Danny to change to an encounter group because he had to get his anger out about the incident. Danny agreed, and

Robert unloaded on me. I sat back and laughed.

Danny stopped him. "You've never had sex with a guy?"

"No."

"Bullshit."

Robert continued with his tirade, and after, Danny told the group that he wanted me to be confronted day and night about my sexuality. Then he looked at me. "Your life is going to be a living hell until you start telling the truth around here."

"I am telling the truth."

"Y'know what? Just shut the fuck up until you're ready to cop to the truth."

After group, I was told to knock on the coordinator's office door and received a haircut for being in denial about my sexuality. That night I got another, and in the morning I got two more. In encounter group the next day, Robert went after me again, but I didn't respond. During the second half of the group I was confronted again about being gay, and I denied it again. Donald called me a liar.

"I'm not here for being gay," I said.

"Then what are you here for?" he asked.

"I don't know. I really don't know."

"You're not going to tell me that you don't belong here, again, are you?"

"No," I said. "I'm telling you that I'm not gay."

"You're a fucking liar."

He spent the entire second half of the group confronting me but I wouldn't tell him what he wanted to hear. As he went on, I could feel the rest of the people in the group start to turn on me. Jane and Gary told me that they didn't believe me, and Robert confronted me with rage. "C'mon, Wayne Kernochan, you're a fucking faggot. Why don't you admit it?"

"Because you're wrong."

Donald interrupted. "So, you're saying Danny is wrong."

That was a loaded question because that was exactly what I was saying, but there was no way I could say that. Donald was a good manipulator, but I was better than him. "I'm not saying anything of the sort."

"Then, you're saying he's right."

"I'm not saying anything about Danny while he's not in the

room…That's against the rules."

"Okay then, I'll go get him."

"Go ahead."

Danny was busy, so Donald continued without him until the end of the group. When it was over, I still hadn't said what they wanted and could see that my fellow residents were getting frustrated by my defiance.

#

Days went by, and Stan pushed me to tell Danny what he wanted to hear. "You're not going anywhere until you do," he said, "so why don't you get it over with?"

"Because it's not true."

"So?"

"Sew buttons."

"Sew buttons?" he asked. "Do you realize what you're doing?"

"Yes."

He shook his head, took a puff of his cigarette and said, "Don't you at least want to smoke again?"

Danny pulled my smoking privilege for 'lollygagging in the kitchen', but that wasn't why he did it. I was the only one doing anything when he walked in. He did it to torture me. I could see the torment wasn't going to end until I told him that I had sex with a man.

"Yeah, I want to smoke again."

"So, say it."

"No."

He laughed, shook his head again and sat down. He opened his notebook, signifying that we were done talking.

#

Promotions were constant because Danny shot so many people down. His hair trigger caused him to have to promote people who had only behaved themselves for a short time. It didn't matter because he would just shoot them down again. Pat Carlson had been shot down, promoted to department head and shot down in the first three weeks I was there.

Mike Calabrese greeted me in the dining room without his costume. "Hey there, fellow service crew member."

"Wow," I said. "Cool for you."

"Danny said if I behave myself for a while, I'll be getting out of here in six months or so."

"Even better."

"C'mon," he said, "let's go have a smoke."

The front porch was open air, so the March wind was unobstructed, making it excruciating. Most people smoked inside the house because of the cold but Mike and I liked it outside because of the serenity. The windows muffled the screaming inside the house.

Outside, Mike said, "Don't do it."

"Don't do what?"

"You're going to be here for two years because that's what the state pays for, no matter what, so don't."

"What the fuck are you talking about?"

"Don't cut off your nose to spite your face," he said. "When they say 'do your thing' they mean 'do our thing'. Tell Danny what he wants to hear and get it over with." He went to the window to see if anyone was listening from the door. "You don't want to do your time here the way I did, believe me."

"Ya know what? I've never been a big fan of 'do what I say, not what I do', so I really don't want to talk about it," I said.

"I'm only looking out for you."

"I know."

"It's only going to get worse."

I knew that too, but didn't care. As afraid as I was of Danny, there were limits to what I could take, and saying I had sex with a man to appease him was over the limit. Besides, there was more to consider—like Robert Gamble.

Where I grew up in New York City, murder wasn't uncommon. Cuckoo Sal—one of the customers from my father's bar—was found in the park up the block from our house dead from a gunshot wound to the head. It wasn't far from where his brother shot and killed a man for making a comment as he kissed a girl on a bench. Later, the brother was shot in the head on Cross Bay Boulevard for going after a gangster with a whiskey bottle. It was a tough neighborhood.

Murderers didn't scare me. A week after Cuckoo Sal stabbed Richie Ebert six times, I played cards with him in the bar. I felt safe in the company of killers, but that wasn't the case with Robert

Gamble. I watched him when he yelled at people and beat them in the ring or with the paddle. He had a mean streak, and he didn't like me, so I was afraid of him.

As creepy as what Matt Brennan had been, I couldn't go to anyone about it because Danny would pin it on me; I was sure of that. I kept it to myself, and kept an eye on Matt. After a few weeks Matt didn't try it again, so I let it go and forgot about it.

In the weeks that followed, Danny pulled my free time and activity privileges, and put me outside to shovel snow. The haircuts continued and the encounter groups got more heated as others jumped on the bandwagon. The only time the pressure eased was when someone acted out and Danny had to deal with them, so the horror I once felt when he abused people turned to relief.

\#

Danny Broach and Cathy Collins became the new target of Danny Bennison's cruelty. Everyone talked about how crazy Danny was from the day he came in, but that didn't stop them from beating and mistreating him. That didn't stop him from acting out and becoming one of Danny Bennison's new projects.

Cathy came in after Danny Broach, and though she was perfectly sane her behavior was as bad. I could see that she hated the physical violence but tolerated it for some reason. I didn't care why because between the two of them I was forgotten.

One day, the expeditors called a general meeting, and the two of them were in opposite corners for breaking one of the cardinal rules: they had sex in the bathroom. Danny Bennison came out with the paddle and gloves, and didn't waste any time. He grabbed two chairs and pulled them to the front of the room.

"Both of you get over the chair."

Cathy smirked as she walked to the front of the room. She stopped in front of the chair, and bent at the knees, like she was curtsying, and when she did, Danny came up behind her and kicked her square in the back. "Get the fuck over the chair," he said, "And, just for that, you get twenties instead of tens."

"I wasn't doing anything," she said.

Danny kicked the chair across the room. "Fuck the chair." He threw her down on the floor. "Pigs belong in the dirt."

By the time the tenth person was done hitting her with the paddle, Cathy's pants had dark blotches on the seat.

"What the fuck is this?" Danny said. He pulled her pants down, and realized that it was blood. "Look at what you did to yourself."

Cathy tried to speak, but couldn't, and Danny didn't let her try to continue. "Shut the fuck up," he said. "I'm going to have to put you in the ring from now until this heals...You're a real piece of work, ya know that?"

"I didn't do nothing."

"You admitted it in group," Danny said. Then he looked at the crowd. "Who wants to go in the ring with this whore?"

Denise McDaniel was first, then Monica Olen, and then Cathy Hogan. They went in order twice, and then Danny declared her 'Bad, Bad, Pig Woman', and told the business crew to make her a sign and a pig costume.

"You're going to sing a song," Danny said.

He gave her the lines one by one, and she practiced for us. "I'm bad, bad, pig woman, da, da, da, da...Watch me play with my tail..."

"Swing it," Danny said. "Swing the tail like it's actually there."

Cathy swung an imaginary tail and sang the song she would have to sing every time she entered or left a room. "I'm bad, bad, pig woman, da, da, da, da...Watch me play with my tail. Because it gives me that, da, da, da, da. I'm bad, bad, pig woman, da, da, da, da. I like you to watch me play with my tail. I'm bad, bad, pig woman, da, da, da, da."

She was contracted to wear pig ears, a nose, and tail, with a prostitute's outfit, and given a sign to wear. After he was done with her, she was sent to the dorm to change, and Danny looked at Danny Broach. "Get up here, you fucking retard."

Danny got up from his chair in the corner and walked to the front of the room. He stood on the balls of his feet and stared at the ceiling. "We're down here, Psycho boy," Danny Bennison said.

Danny Broach smirked at that.

"Ya know what?" Danny Bennison said. "I forgot all about you." He pulled the chair to Danny Broach. "Get over the chair."

He did, and Danny had the men beat him with the paddle. He didn't make a sound, but his smile went away, and by the fourth set of ten his face screwed up in agony. Tears came to his eyes.

When it was done, Danny Bennison put him in the ring and shot him down.

Throughout the beating, he called Danny Broach crazy ten different ways. Psycho boy was his favorite, but he called him a nut job, a mental case, and stone cold fucking crazy. When he was beaten and subdued, Danny asked him about all the mental institutions he had been in.

"I don't remember them all."

"So, you're that fucking psycho, that you lost count," Danny Bennison said. "That's sad."

"It was because of the wine," Danny Broach said. "It's always because of the wine." Then, he told us that he was a homeless wino, and that he got in trouble whenever he had money. Danny and Donald injected jokes, and the house had a good laugh at Danny Broach's expense. He smiled at one of Donald's jokes, and said, "One time, I had five dollars and a bottle of Old Crow."

Donald stopped him. "Five dollars and a bottle of Old Crow? How would you like five knuckles and another round in the ring?"

The smile went away. Danny Bennison said, "This isn't your birthday party, Psycho boy. This is a general meeting."

"Yeah," Donald said. "We're not laughing with you. We're laughing at you."

Danny ended the G.M. by giving Danny Broach a hobo costume, and a sign explaining why, and sent him to the dorm to change into shorts. Then he gave the house a twenty minute lecture about how bad the house's attitude was, and dismissed us.

#

"Danny Broach had it coming." Gary Ross said to Mike and me afterward. "He's been pushing everyone's buttons since he got here."

"Yeah, but he's seriously crazy," I said.

"Uh huh, and he better knock it off, before he gets some real pain."

"I don't think he's sane enough to realize that."

"The ring knocked the crazy out of him."

"Yeah, but for how long?" Mike said.

Gary shrugged.

Chapter 5

Spring brought Maine to life. The snow white and pine green colors gave way to red and blue wildflowers and grass replaced the icy paths we traveled in winter. It was as beautiful as Doctor Peck said. Birds came to wake us in the morning and life rose from the muddy earth, brilliantly disguising the horror of Poland Springs.

On April 25th, 1978, Saint Paul, Minnesota repealed its gay rights ordinance after Anita Bryant succeeded with her anti-gay campaign in Dade County, Florida. She was satisfied with taking gay people's rights away, but my director wasn't. Danny's anti-gay campaign was more violent—he wanted to beat the gay out of them. His homophobia was loud and proud, and the pressure on me continued.

I was shamed constantly for being a liar and not sharing about my feelings. Danny and Donald got angrier as time went by because I accepted whatever punishment they gave me and didn't give them a reason to beat the truth out of me. I stayed quiet, cleaned floors and took the humiliation without a word.

Stan and Mike pushed me to tell the lie that Danny wanted to hear, but I wouldn't do it. Eventually, they began to get angry about my stubbornness. "I can't help you if you refuse to help yourself," Stan said. "This is getting stupid."

"Yeah," Mike said. "This is getting ridiculous."

"What's ridiculous is that I have to lie to get ahead in this place."

"Injustices are part of the program," Mike said. "You just have to deal with them."

Stan nodded.

\#

May brought more job changes. Mike had behaved himself on the service crew for a few weeks so he was promoted to department head of the kitchen. Stan was made coordinator of the service crew. Lisa Groton and Jane Tolar were promoted to the kitchen crew and Danny Broach and Cathy Collins were taken off shot-down and put back on the service crew.

Danny left me on the service crew because he was determined to make me admit to being gay. I didn't mind because I saw that having responsibility brought more attention to the person with it, and the last thing I wanted was the attention of staff. Danny had replaced my father as the person I most wanted to get away from.

On May 5th, Pete Rose got his three-thousandth hit as a Cincinnati Red but we didn't see it because the house had lost its TV privilege. The harder Danny beat on people, the worse their behavior became. I wasn't the only one defying our terrorist leader.

The pressure on me dissipated over the months, and the new focus of staff became about my intellect. One night in school, during a lecture about the ocean, Mister Dionne started looking in a book for the weight of water. "I forget what it is," he said.

"Isn't it, like, sixty-two pounds per square foot?" I said.

He stopped. "How the hell did you know that?"

"I don't know."

He pointed to the page he was searching. "Well, it's actually sixty two point four pounds per square foot. But who's counting."

The class laughed, and my fellow residents marveled about how smart I was for a few days, but then Danny turned my newfound fame against me. Whenever I did something wrong after that, he had me blasted in haircuts for thinking I was smarter than everyone else, and being a know-it-all. The encounter group anger followed the theme. What people liked me for a week prior turned into the reason why everyone hated me. The new focus made me forget about the incident with Matt Brennan until it happened again.

#

There were three people in the house in positions of authority that I trusted. Wayne Weaver and Yvette Portella were nice to me, but I didn't feel comfortable telling either of them. Mike Calabrese and I had a contract. We talked about the program negatively, and that was a big rule to break, so I trusted him. Everyone ratted themselves out, which was called 'copping to your guilt' and if someone had a crisis of conscience and ratted you out, you were dealt with more harshly than they were. I went to Mike the next morning.

"Matt Brennan was looking at me, and jerking off, last night."

"Really?"

"Yeah, man, but here's the embarrassing part...I was jerking off when he did it."

"Okay," Mike said. "That's kinda weird."

"I stopped when I saw him...I'm not a fag....you gotta help me, man."

Mike said, "Danny's been after you, so he ain't gonna take your word for it."

That was a fact, but Mike had a plan. "If I catch him doing it, then you have a witness, and Danny has to believe you."

"What do you want me to do?"

"I'll watch from the door, and you get him to do it, then we've got him."

It was a strange request, but everything about Élan was strange, so I agreed to it.

#

That night, when everything settled down and the men were asleep, I pretended to jerk off, and Matt took the bait. He started doing it with me, like we were doing it together. When he did, Mike waved to me, and I sat up. Then he stepped inside and turned on the light. "You're a fucking pervert, Matt Brennan. I can't believe this shit."

Matt yelled. "What the fuck are you talking about?"

"I saw you looking at him, ya pervert. What are ya trying to do? Get him to do it with you?"

By that time, Dave Winston was in the room. "What the fuck is going on in here?"

Mike explained as Matt protested, so Dave said, "Matt, be quiet until Mike is done, and then you'll have your say."

"But this is bullshit."

"I said to be quiet."

"But, this is a fucking lie."

"Shut up, Matt."

"No, I'm not going to shut up."

Dave took him into the bathroom, then came out alone, and told Mike to go up to Élan Three to ask the director on duty what to do. Mike went, and Dave got everyone settled back into bed.

In the morning, Matt was sitting in the corner, and I was

relieved. After breakfast, they called a general meeting and we were herded into the dining room to sit and wait. Eventually, Danny came out, carrying the bag and the paddle. "Get up here," he said.

He was looking at me.

\#

I had just let out my breath, I remember, because I couldn't get another for a few seconds. When air finally filled my lungs, the panic kicked in.

"I said get the fuck up here," he yelled.

I got to the front of the room as fast as I could. Danny didn't throw me against the wall, so I relaxed slightly. He didn't seem as angry as usual.

"Get up here," he yelled, looking at Mike Calabrese.

Mike shrugged, put out his arms, and pointed the palms of his hands to the sky. "What did I do?"

Danny sneered. "You fucking faggot, get up here."

Mike moved as fast as I did but Danny cut him off and threw him against the wall again. I was confused. Danny turned to the house. "Who's got something to say to these two?"

The shot-downs were the only ones that didn't charge us. More than twenty people stood inches from me, screaming profanity in my ears and face, spitting into both. Through it, the thing that bothered me most was that they had no idea what they were yelling at me for.

When they were done, Danny addressed Mike. "So, what the fuck is going on here, Michael?"

Mike told the story up to the idea of busting Matt watching me as I jerked off, and Danny started laughing. It was an evil laugh. The house could sense that Danny wanted blood, and I could see that he wanted it more from Mike than me. Danny didn't like him even when he was a department head.

"Do you expect me to believe this bullshit?" Danny said. "You two faggots are gonna try and put this whole thing on Matt Brennan?"

"I'm not a faggot," I said.

"Shut your fucking mouth. I wasn't talking to you."

I lowered my head.

For the next hour they beat on Mike until he admitted that he had set the whole thing up to get off on Matt and I jerking off together. It wasn't true, and the crowd knew from the amount of punishment it took that Mike said it to appease Danny. I watched in horror, waiting my turn, like Danny in his prison cell waiting to be raped.

Though I was afraid, I was calm, and considered my options. My father was heavy handed and I was from a tough neighborhood, so I got my share of beatings. There was no way I was going to admit that I was a willing participant in what happened, so it was going to be a severe one.

"And, you," Danny said. "This is how you get your rocks off? By setting up this asshole?" He pointed to Matt.

"I wasn't the one." I pointed to Matt. "He was the one that started this...He's the fag, not me."

Danny looked at Matt. "Is this true?"

Matt shook his head. "That's a lie."

Danny looked confused for a second. "Ya know what? I don't know who to believe here," He looked at Donald. "Do you?"

Donald said, "I don't believe either of them. I think they're both faggots."

"Well, people at Vitam have told me that this isn't the first time you've been suspected of being a fruit, Wayne, so I'm leaning in Matt Brennan's direction."

"I'm the one that came to staff."

"Your friend Kip says hi."

That was what it was about. Vitam had given information to Élan to use against me, and the thing that got Danny's attention was Kip Neville's assessment that I was gay. Considering the circumstance, it didn't look good for me.

"Kip was wrong about me."

"That man has worked with people like you for years," Danny said. "As a matter of fact, he sounded like a faggot himself. C'mon, dude, admit it...you enjoyed this."

"No, I didn't, Danny. I swear to you, I'm not gay."

"Only faggots use the word gay, dude. Get the fuck out of here."

Danny wasn't happy not getting the answers that he wanted, but there was a ring of truth to my story, and everyone sensed it. Danny couldn't ignore it. "Y'know what?" he said. "I'm going to shoot the both of you down until the truth comes out. You two work it out. I don't have time for this shit."

And that was it. No ring or paddle. I hadn't seen anyone refuse to admit to something the staff wanted in a general meeting without one or the other, or both. Danny had serious doubts about Matt Brennan or my fate would have been worse.

After the general meeting, I was taken to the men's dorm to change into a pair of shorts. Danny also had them make me a sign. It was about how smart I was. It said 'my name is Wayne, but people call me Mister Know-it-all. Please ask me why I need to feel better than everyone because of my low self-esteem'.

The sign was three feet wide, four feet long, and hung to the middle of my shins. It had a strap made of twisted plastic wrap that dug into my neck. It was heavy and cumbersome which was going to make my new position hell, since shot-downs spent most of the day scrubbing floors between haircuts and groups.

By lunch my knees were sore and by dinner they were in agony, yet scrubbing floors on my knees was my favorite part of the day. Encounter groups and haircuts were just a way for people to unload their anger, and Robert Gamble took full advantage of it. He began using the word faggot in haircuts, which I hadn't seen done before.

Because they didn't have drugs or crimes to base their therapy on, haircuts were about topics. The coordinators believed that Matt was the one who initiated the incident that got me shot-down, so the haircuts were about me being a know-it-all, but Robert spun it into me thinking I was smart enough to hide my homosexuality. He sat on the end of his chair like he wanted to jump up and hit me, and screamed angrily.

\#

That night in encounter group, when Donald said, "Go," I went, and when I did, the frustration of the past three months came out. I sat at the edge of my chair and spewed profanity at Matt, as he did the same.

In the middle, I considered jumping up and punching him in the face because he was accusing me of lying to get him in trouble; I could see that he was never going to admit to what he did, and that we were going to be shot down forever, but physical violence was dealt with severely. I was lucky that Danny didn't use the ring or paddle on me earlier at the general meeting, so I stayed at the edge of my chair until I was done.

When we were done, Mike Calabrese went after Matt, and I sat back. There was a rush that steadily increased as I yelled at Matt, and when I was done it was replaced by calm. It was the first time I had unloaded on someone, and it felt good.

I was becoming like them.

Chapter 6

The warm temperatures brought outside activities, but Matt and I scrubbed floors and cleaned toilets, watching the deserving residents have fun through the dining room window. Even the shot-downs were allowed outside to clean. Danny wanted Matt or me to confess and our lack of one wasn't wearing him down.

It was an encounter group that got me my next general meeting. The months of insanity and degradation had finally gotten to me. I was screaming at Matt about what I would do to him if we were out there, when he yelled something about me setting him up, and I snapped. I jumped up, out of my chair, got in his face, and said "Stop fucking saying that!"

Danny was observing the group from the kitchen, smoking a cigarette and drinking a cup of coffee. Jumping out of your seat while confronting someone was considered provoking physical violence, so when it happened he put down his cigarette, and said, "Oh, hell no…General Meeting!"

I sat down, but he said, "No, you get in front of the room."

I did.

#

The house was seated in the dining room in thirty-four seconds; I knew that because I stared at the clock on the dining room wall and counted. When they were seated and the expeditors had a correct headcount, Danny said "Who wants to go in the ring with this tough guy?"

Everyone in a position of authority was expected to raise their hand, that was quietly understood, so I knew Allen, George and Dave raised their hands for that reason, but Robert Gamble waved his like he wanted blood; it was in his eyes, so Danny picked him first.

"First you…" Then he pointed at George and Allen. "…Then you, and you."

Donald said, "Why don't we let the house get their feelings off while we lace up the gloves?"

"That's a capital idea, my friend." Danny said.

They laughed.

Donald said to the house, "Who has feelings for this fucking homo?"

It wasn't the screaming or spitting that bothered me, it was the anger. Some of the spitting was on purpose so it wasn't therapy, it was hate. I hadn't done anything to the residents of Élan Seven but they charged me like I was the one who killed an innocent man. I stared straight ahead, but watched Donald and Robert out of the corner of my eye. They were smiling.

Robert was older, bigger and stronger than me. He looked like the kind of guy who could beat a man to death. My fear went away because I knew Danny wasn't going to stop the beating until I was beat. I accepted that and stood with my hands at my sides.

"The Marquis of Queensbury rules are in place," Danny said. "No kicking, biting or hitting below the belt…Ding"

There wasn't an actual bell, so Danny said the word ding. A real bell would have been preferable because it's mechanical. Danny's voice was emotional, and the emotion was joy. I could see that he had been dying to get me in this position because he didn't like how I would endure his torture rather than say he was right.

We wore headgear but it did little good. Robert went straight for my face, and I let him. When he saw that I was being defiant by keeping my hands at my side, he hit me three times fast, which rattled all thought from my brain. The world turned static-white, like a TV screen that lost its picture. When it cleared he hit me twice more. When I was able to think again, and didn't raise my hands to defend myself, he backed off looking confused.

He drew his fist back and went for the face again, but this time I sidestepped him and the force of his swing made him lose his balance. He fell to his knees and looked embarrassed as he got up, so I knew that he wanted to go for the face again. Then I covered up like Mike and Debbie had done, and let him beat on my back and sides. When my head cleared again, I turned and faced him. He hit me a few more times, but Danny said ding, and the round was over.

I covered up to let George Rees and Allen Kelly hit my back and sides, and then Danny put me over a chair, and picked girls to hit me with the paddle. When that was done, I was afraid to ask to see the nurse. I swallowed the blood in my mouth and forced myself to stand in front of the room.

"So, you're getting frustrated, huh, Mister Know-It-All?"

The crowd murmured so Danny let them charge me again, and when they were done he got back to my situation with Matt. "I'm going to get a confession out of one of you, so get used to this shit." He lit a cigarette. "What the fuck were you thinking, anyway?"

"I wasn't"

"You bet your ass, you weren't."

"Danny, I wasn't the one that started this…"

"Oh, bullshit."

"Do you really think I'm stupid enough to do that after what Kip Neville told you?"

"Kip Neville says you're gay."

"Kip Neville is a faggot; even you said it Danny. He said that shit because I wouldn't let him touch me."

It was a lie, but it played into Danny's homophobia, and it worked from the look on his face. "I knew that guy had a fag voice." He smiled. "So, he hit on you?"

I told Danny that Kip threatened me when I thwarted his advances, but I told him to go fuck himself, and that was the reason I acted out and made Vitam throw me out. Danny believed me and lightened up when he was convinced that I was a homophobe like him.

#

The coordinators continued to provoke me, but it became about other things. They latched onto Danny's new title -- Mister Know-it –all -- and everything I did wrong was either because I thought I was smarter than everyone or smart enough to get away with it. When I did something clumsy I got yelled at for not being as smart as I thought I was. It got boring quickly.

One day, Mike Calabrese said, "Why are you such a smart ass, anyway?"

"Ya mean, why do I think I'm smarter than everyone here?"

"Yeah."

"Because I am."

He laughed. "Maybe you're smarter than these mother

fuckers," he said, "but not me. I'm one step ahead of you kid."

"You're the one that got us in this mess."

Mike got angry. "Matt Brennan got us into this and don't you forget it. I was trying to help you."

It had been so long that I forgot that. "Sorry, pal."

"It's alright."

#

When the haircuts weren't about me being Mister Know-it-all, they were a cheap attempt at therapy. Mine were usually about being abandoned by my father, and how that made me sexually inadequate, which was going to lead me back to drugs, none of which was true.

That night, Yvette Portella told me to knock on the expeditor's door during the evening clean up, so I did.

"Who's out there?"

"Wayne."

"Come in!"

I did.

"Do you know why you're standing there?"

"No."

A haircut was usually done by a coordinator, a department head and a peer, and was given in angry melody. The person yelling took a deep breath and screamed in a singsong manner. "Uh, ya, don't know..." then, he would take another deep breath... "uh, what your problem is..." then another deep breath... "but you think you can walk around here..." big breath... "acting like a know it all..." It varied in intensity and melody, but everyone did it, and they usually finished by telling you that if you think you're going to continue doing what you're doing 'you've got another think coming'.

George Rees told me that he hung a man with a telephone wire at the age of fifteen, but he didn't seem like a cold blooded killer, so I liked him. Allen Kelly was the department head, and I liked him because, despite the fact he was strict, he was fair. In lieu of a peer, they had Robert Gamble who was still angry that I beat him in the ring.

George yelled at me for being manipulative, which was valid. He liked me and tried to be constructive, so I listened, and when he was done, I turned to Allen. He covered the, Mister Know-It-All angle of my disrespect and was constructive as well. When he was done, I turned to Robert Gamble, who wouldn't let the gay thing go.

Robert didn't like that I took his best and didn't cower, so his hatred for me got worse. He yelled at me for not admitting that I was gay, and said that if I didn't get it out in the open, I was going to go back to drugs, and end up on the streets again. When he was done, I said "I've never done drugs."

None of them spoke for a second. George looked confused, and Allen fought back a smirk, but Robert stood up and shouted. "Go back out, and knock on that door."

I did.

When I reentered the room, they blasted me for talking back in a haircut. George and Allen were stern and angry but Robert was livid. When he was done, I said, "I'm sorry to all of you for the disrespect." They didn't say anything, so I continued. "I should have corrected you after the haircut."

"Get out and knock on that door again," George Rees said.

I did.

"Who's out there?"

"Wayne."

"Come in!"

I didn't know Danny was in his office and could hear everything. When I reentered the room, he was standing next to the door. "You don't correct my expeditors, Mister Know-it all." He walked up to me. "They worked hard to get where they are." He spat as he screamed. "So you show them some fucking respect!"

He pointed to the door, "Now, get the fuck out of here!"

On my way out the door, I heard him tell George to call a general meeting.

#

Danny seemed done with me, and changed the tone of voice when he spoke to George, so I knew the G.M. was for something else. We all knew there was something up because the business office had the door closed for hours and was working on something for Danny.

George came out of the coordinator's office, pointed to the business office door, then looked at Wayne Weaver. "Tell them we're ready." Then he turned to Mike Calabrese, Gary Ross, and

48

Pat Carlson. "You three get in front of the room."

There had been a test in school the night before which determined our final grade; Mike, Gary and Pat had failed it. Danny gave them signs and dunce caps to wear, and threatened them. He berated Mike and Gary, telling them they were going to end up in prison as soon as they left Élan. Pat Carlson stood quietly through it all.

Pat was my friend. He was funny and nice, and had an innocent face. He wasn't hard or street-worn like the rest of them. He didn't fit in, so I commiserated with him. When Danny was done with Mike and Gary, he put a dunce cap on Pat and had the house yell and spit on him. Then he told Pat to tell the house why he was in Élan.

Pat looked down at the ground.

"Look at them," Danny shouted. "Tell these people what the fuck you're here for."

"I took a kid into the woods..."

"What was his name?" Danny said. "He had a fucking name."

"His name is Lucky."

"No," Danny said. "His name 'was' Lucky. Go on and tell your peers what you did to Lucky."

Pat told us that he took Lucky—an eight-year-old boy—into the woods to molest him, then freaked out and killed him. When he was done with the story, Danny said, "How did you kill him?"

"I hit him in the head with a rock."

Danny stood up and got in Pat's face. "What else did you do?" he said. "Don't make me pry every detail out of you."

Pat told us that he knocked Lucky down, beat his head in with a rock, kicked him and stuck a laundry pin through his heart. Then he covered him with leaves and left him there. The house was as horrified by the way he told the story as the story itself. He spoke in a monotone, like he was describing a day at work.

"Tell them what the doctor said to you," Danny said.

"He said I would never get better."

"He said that you'd do it again, didn't he?"

"Yeah."

"Yeah?" Danny shook his head. "You have no emotion in your voice at all. What the fuck is wrong with you?"

Pat then told us that his psychiatrist considered him a

sociopath, and expected that he would kill again and again. Danny added quotes from his file as he told the story. Finally, Danny said, "Does anyone have any feelings about this?" It was the first time I joined in.

Danny put Pat in the ring. I wondered what good it would do; Pat was a serial killer and Élan's abuse was only going to make him worse. When he was done with Pat, Danny addressed the anger in the house. "This house is more out of control than I thought it could ever get," he said, "so I'm starting a new department." He handed Wayne Weaver a piece of paper. "I'm going to remove the cancer from this house."

There were over four hundred incident reports in the month of June, so Danny initiated the cancer crew. "The area behind the house is your new home. You'll eat, drink and piss out there. I can't have you people infecting everyone."

Wayne called off names, and the new crew stepped forward. Mike Calabrese, Matt Brennan, Pat Carlson and Donna Fosche were called in that order. My name was called last.

Chapter 7

Summer brought more foliage, bright colors, deer, bear and moose; it was easy to see them from my new location. Rain or shine, we went from the dorm to the back of the house, where we ate our meals and cleared brush until the house went to sleep. We were deemed not worthy of therapy, so it was the most serene of all my months at Élan. I loved it immediately.

The dead trees and brush behind the house were thick, with the designated dump ground two-hundred yards away; there was enough work to keep the four of us busy for a year. It went slowly for the first week but picked up as people were added to our ranks. Gary Ross and Cathy Collins came first, followed by Danny Broach and Mark Strickland.

\#

July brought a tight house because Stan Wasicki split with Mark Strickland. For Danny, that was the last straw. When they were brought back a week later, the house was called into the dining room for a general meeting.

"Isn't this nice?" Danny said. Then he looked at them. "We missed you boys."

Donald said, "We hardly slept from worry."

Danny laughed.

Donald said to Danny "Shouldn't we let the house have their say?"

Danny nodded and looked to the house. "What do you people have to say to these two?"

The screamers and spitters had plenty of anger for them. Splitees got themselves extra worked up. I didn't understand that because any one of them would do it if they thought they could get away with it. When they were done, Danny said "So, you guys got all the way to Connecticut, did ya?"

Mark tried to speak, but Danny cut him off, and addressed Stan. "I don't want to hear from the shot-down. I want to hear from his coordinator. You fucking asshole, this is how you repay me for giving you a position in this house?"

Stan looked at the ground.

"Look at me."

He looked up. Stan and Mark had made fun of the program with their friends while they were gone. Mark had told us that they gave their friends haircuts and had mock encounter groups, as Danny gritted his teeth.

"So, that's what you're doing with the person you were in charge of?" Danny asked Stan.

"Yeah."

"Who wants to go in the ring with this disgrace?"

They beat Stan first, then Mark. Danny was as angry as I'd seen him. He made Mark tell us about his experiences as a male prostitute, and accused him and Stan of having a gay relationship. When they wouldn't admit it, he had them beaten some more. When he was finished, he looked to the house "This place is out of control," he said. "From this second on, this is a tight house."

Mike Calabrese had told me about tight houses and it sounded like a nightmare. As Danny explained the rules, he collected everyone's cigarettes and threw them in the garbage. No one was allowed to speak without permission, and that was requested by raising your hand.

"Anything you do," Danny said, "even if you have to piss, you get permission from expeditors. Do you people fucking understand me!"

We nodded.

"Good, because if anyone says a fucking word, they're going in the ring."

Everyone was shot down except the expeditors and all activities and groups were off. Except for school, we were to clean. All privileges were pulled. Coordinators would be brought down from Élan Three. Danny followed that by telling us what an embarrassment we were to him in front of other houses. "And, if any of you have the audacity to speak, or talk back to one of them, you're fucking dead!"

\#

Haircuts were done anywhere you were standing. We knocked on poles, walls and mailboxes. The first day, Matt Brennan knocked on a broom. The normal insanity of Élan became an all-day screamfest. In the first two hours, there were three general meetings. Mike Calabrese had spoken so Danny put him in the ring, Danny Broach laughed so he was spanked, then Cathy Collins got both for talking back to Donald.

When the third G.M. was over, Danny threw the lunch trays into the garbage. "You fucking people don't deserve lunch." Then he kicked the garbage can over, and dragged it across the dining room spreading trash from one end to the other. "Clean that up…and don't let me catch you eating any of it."

Donald took a bite of a sandwich and told the expeditors. "It's very good, so keep an eye on the fat fucks."

We spent the day cleaning up behind Danny and Donald as they threw garbage around the house. It got more disgusting each time. They were having fun with it. Danny poured five gallons of oil on the floor of the kitchen and laughed as we fell down. I said nothing, and scrubbed the kitchen floor with Yolanda Cruz.

By day three the house began to smell like garbage, yet Danny and Donald wouldn't stop. Yolanda and I were up to our ankles in four-day-old food when we found the maggots. It wasn't announced, but the garbage throwing ended.

The former cancer crew were kept awake all night and denied food. When I got tired I ate sugar packets from a box under the kitchen counter. Yolanda elbowed me. "Give me some."

I handed her some. "Don't fucking get caught with this."
#
Day four of the tight house was dedicated to Mary Jones. I was told that 'Mary is Mary' when I asked why she was allowed to do whatever she wanted. George Rees told me that she was crazy and Joe Ricci liked her, so she was allowed.

Mary was childlike and funny, so I liked her. She liked me, and flirted with me. When Donna Bouton asked me why Mary was allowed to come and go as she pleased, I told her what I was told. "Mary is Mary."

Joe Ricci knew that Mary would never conform to the rigor of the program, so he approved her unrestrained comings and goings. If it had been anyone but her, people would have protested, but it was Mary so no one was bothered by it. If they were, they didn't say anything.

Right before dinner, a general meeting was called and she was in the corner, so the house went silent. Whatever it was, it was sure to be bad. Mary grabbed the men's genitals in front of staff; I couldn't imagine what she did to be given a G.M.

"What the fuck did you do?" Danny said, as he came out of his office. "What the fuck did you do up there?" He pointed up the hill, to Élan Three.

Mary was in one of her manic states, but it wasn't one of the playful ones. "I didn't do anything. I was just trying to see Joe Ricci."

"Joe said he didn't want to see you today, and that he'd see you tomorrow."

"Yeah, but…"

"Yeah, but, my ass," Danny cut her off. "You disrespected Joe, Peter, and this house, so your days of running around, and doing what you want are over." He pulled a chair next to her. "Get over the chair."

"But, Danny…"

"Get over the chair!" he yelled.

"But, I wasn't doing anything."

Danny grabbed at her, but Mary avoided him. He righted himself, grabbed her and tried to put her over the chair, but she fought him and he missed, so they both went down to the ground. Danny got up, and called the expeditors to help him.

"You fat piece of shit…We'll just do this on the floor." He handed the paddle to Denise. "Tan her fucking ass."

For two hours they beat Mary, wearing her down a little at a time. She screamed and cried, becoming hysterical. Danny continued, "Ten…Ten more…Next. Ten…Ten more... Next…"

I was happy to be shot-down and unable to participate. Everyone but us had to spank her at least once. When Mary was beaten, Danny shot her down and told Yvette Portella and Denise McDaniel to take her to the dorm to change into shorts.

"From now on you're just another piece of shit from Élan Seven like these pieces of shit." He pointed to us. "So, get used to it."

#

When Mary was gone, Danny promoted the ex-coordinators back to their positions. Dave, Denise, George and Allen were restored to their jobs without privileges. Those were never coming back, according to Danny.

"Most of you people will graduate without ever having a smoke or a cup of coffee," he said

#

When the general meeting was over, the house went to bed. The cancer crew stayed behind to clean the house before we were allowed to sleep. The night man from Élan Three was Mike Skakel. Mike Calabrese told me that he was related to the Kennedy family and had killed his girlfriend in a drunken rage. When I stayed in Élan Three for a day when I first arrived, he wore a sign that said 'Ask me why I killed my next door neighbor', so I believed it and didn't like him.

Mike wore a wool overcoat. It looked good on him, but was strange for someone our age to wear. Leather was the style. He said "The sooner you're done, the sooner you get to go to bed, so make it quick."

Dave was the coordinator of the expeditors, and spent most of his time working with Danny or the other coordinators. He came into the dining room and looked at Wayne Weaver, who was writing in a notebook. "What are you up to, my man?"

"I'm doing the new dorm room assignments," Wayne said.

Dave pointed to me. "Put this guy in my room...I like him."

Mike looked up from his paperwork. "Really?"

"Yeah, he's a good guy....Listen, I gotta go."

Dave left, and Wayne went into the coordinators office, so I raised my hand.

"Yeah," Mike said.

"Can I use the bathroom?"

"Go ahead, but make it quick, huh?"

Dave was well liked, so his endorsement of me had an effect on Mike. He was nice to me. I expected that being related to the Kennedy clan would make him aloof, but it didn't. I went to the bathroom and came back.

Mike put away his clipboard and papers. "What happened to you a few months ago, with Matt Brennan?"

I explained the story as I washed the dishes. Mike listened but he looked like he wanted to interrupt me, so I stopped. "What?"

"I know the story, dude. I mean, what's with not copping to

it?" he said. "Why don't you just do it, and get these people off your back already?"

"Because I'm not gay, and he was the one that started it."

"Why should anyone believe you?"

"If I was gay, I'd have better taste in men."

Mike laughed. "I see your point, but Dude, for real, tell them what they want to hear or you're going to be here for a long time."

"I don't care."

He shook his head. "You'll care after you've been here a year; you'll care more when you've been here two. Tell these people what they want to hear...everyone does, eventually."

Then he told me that the story about him killing his neighbor was a lie, and that he was forced to say it. "Why should anyone believe you?" I asked.

"Exactly," he said.

"Sorry, I aint gonna do it."

"Then you're going to be a miserable person for a long time."

I knew that.

"Why don't you go out for football?"

I turned to him. "Are shot-downs allowed?"

"That's what I hear."

Gary and Mike told me about the problems Joe Ricci was having getting Élan into a school football program. Mike told me that Joe was trying to make Élan look like a school, but that the people in surrounding towns saw us as a lunatic asylum.

The bias was understandable. When people considered why we were there, and combined it with the behavior of splitees when they were on the lam, they had legitimate concerns. People didn't want their kids playing with us, and I didn't blame them.

"Then, I'm there," I said. "Anything, is better than this."

Mike told me not to get too excited, because there was going to be house structure. The coordinators would give haircuts and talking to's, and that we would be promoted and shot down like any other day at Élan.

"Plus," he said, "Football is going to be hell."

"Not worse than this place."

He laughed. "You guys are pretty fucking out of control."

"The fruit don't fall far from the tree."

Mike looked to see if anyone heard me. "Anyway...Sign-up is

next Monday. Be there, huh?"

#

Mary was still Mary, and a tight house didn't change that, so that night we were woken by the shouts. "General meeting."

I had just fallen asleep, so my head began to spin. I raised my hand.

"Yes, Wayne Kernochan," Robert Gamble said.

"May I use the bathroom?"

"Go ahead. You have two minutes."

Inside the bathroom, I faced the brick wall, steadied myself, and gritted my teeth. Then, I rammed my head against the brick as hard as I could. The pain went down my spine into my back. I hit the ground but didn't lose consciousness. It wasn't long before Robert come looking for me. "What the hell are you doing, Wayne Kernochan?"

"I passed out and hit the wall, man."

"Knock on that wall, Wayne Kernochan."

"I can't stand up."

He made me knock with my back against the wall, and blasted me for lying on the bathroom floor. That got Dave's attention, so he came in and told Robert to get someone to help me to my bed.

#

I slept as Danny spent three hours beating Mary Jones, and didn't wake when the men returned to the dorm. In the morning my head was on fire, but I didn't care. It was the same as when Robert beat me in the ring. The fear was gone. Pain was easier to deal with than that. For me, pain was the only thing that was real. It was becoming like medicine.

Chapter 8

By August, the tight house was loosened up and most people had privileges back. The cancer crew was disbanded and reintegrated into the house as shot-downs. Football practice was open to anyone in the house regardless of position. Joe Ricci wanted to see all willing men on the practice field on August 1st. Every male from Élan Seven showed. I was obviously not the only one tired of the daily grind.

"We get Sunday brunch meals every day of the week," Mike Calabrese said. "The football team eats well if nothing else."

"And we're out of this fucking place," Gary Ross said. "Don't forget that."

"And we'll be outside," I said.

Mike checked to see if anyone could hear us. "Getting away from Danny, I'd do anything for that."

#

Joe Ricci, Peter McCann and Marty Kruglick greeted us on the practice field and had us sit in rows with our houses. The first order of business was to tell us how badly we would be beaten if one of us decided to try to split while we were on the road for a game.

"You'll pray for it to stop," Joe said. "But it won't."

"And you'll tack two years onto your stay here," Marty added.

Then Peter told us that football was going to be the same as the house. Haircuts and punishments would be dealt with by the team. He pointed to George White, the biggest guy there. "Stand up." He did, and Joe said "Do you guys really want to go in the ring with him?"

Everyone laughed, some of us nervously.

We spent an hour sorting out uniforms, and another picking our positions. I chose defensive end because Joe wanted faster guys there. I was sure I could do well. When that was sorted out, we split up into groups of ten and did calisthenics.

By lunch we were tired, but it was a good tired. I picked a spot under the trees to eat and spent the time watching the guys play soccer. They were as tired as the rest of us, but wanted to keep busy. I wanted to join in but didn't know them, so I ate my lunch and watched from the sideline.

The men from Parsonsfield were as rough looking as the guys from our house; some of them looked even worse. George White was as Mike Calabrese described him, 'a giant gorilla'. He was dark black, the size of a professional football player, and there wasn't an ounce of fat on his body. He was imposing.

Larry Rhodes was Robert Gamble's partner. They decided one day to kill a man for being gay. Both claimed that he hadn't touched either of them. Danny suspected that was a lie. He asked about it all the time.

Robert was the only guy from our house to play soccer, which was why I wasn't heartbroken about not being included. He and Larry were standoffish towards each other which made me assume they were told not to fraternize.

Wayne Weaver was our biggest guy. He was muscular, very athletic. He was going to be a halfback. It was clear from doing laps earlier that he was going to be our star. "What are you thinking about?" he asked.

"It's gonna really suck going back to the house after this."

He laughed at my candor. "Yeah, probably...so enjoy it."

I rolled over onto my back and laced my fingers behind my head. "I think I will."

#

After lunch we all had uniforms that fit. We spent most of the session hitting the blocking dummies and pushing the sled. I positioned myself into the first line to hit the team sled because I wanted to hit it with George White and Wayne Weaver. We hit awkwardly—one side hit a second before the other, and my shoulder snapped. I knew it was bad.

When I grabbed it, Marty saw that I was in pain. "Hey, number twenty two, are you okay?"

"Just a little rattled. I'm okay."

It was fucked, but I wasn't going to tell him that. An injury would land me back in the house, and that was worse than pain so I shook it off, and got back in line. "Let's go, ladies," I yelled

\#

Back at the house the topic was Mary Jones, the subject was behavior. As I suspected, Mary couldn't be tamed. When she wasn't manic, she was lucid and well behaved. When she was manic, she acted out. Danny was getting frustrated because adhering to the rules kept her in a manic state.

After dozens of spankings, it was clear she wanted to be abused, because she deliberately provoked Danny. She needed a doctor. I wasn't the only one that saw it.

Mike Calabrese said she was crazy. "All the pain in the world is not going to change that!"

"You'd think that something would get through to her brain," I said.

Mike jerked his head in the direction of Danny's office. "You'd think something would get through to his."

\#

I was lucky that it was my left shoulder, because I was still capable of getting my work done. My greatest fear was that someone was going to notice me favoring it and send me to the nurse. That problem was solved the next day when every football player woke up with sore muscles. They limped and complained, so I blended in.

For the next week it was easy to disguise my injury, but it didn't get better so I knew that my time on the field was limited. I enjoyed it while it lasted. I was finally sidelined on a Friday lunch break while playing soccer.

I tried to stop the ball by stepping on it, but misjudged the ball, and fell to the ground, landing on my knee. It would have been okay if I landed on the grass, but my knee met a rock, there was a crunch, and my football career was over.

"You're on restricted duty, and off the football team." the Nurse said.

"What if it gets better?"

"It won't be better this year."

I was sent back to the insanity.

\#

Mary Jones was in the corner when I got to the house. I was instructed to sit in the dining room with my leg up on a chair. I was ten feet away from her. "What happened to you?"

Yvette Portella was her P.O. "Don't talk to her."

I shrugged at Mary. "Sorry."

"Oh, it's okay. I'm going to get a general meeting in a few minutes. What more trouble can I get in?"

"Mary Jones, be quiet," Yvette said.

"What for?"

"How about to make me look good?"

Mary stopped. "Okay. For you I'll do it."

"Thank you."

Mary looked at the wall, so Yvette turned to me. "So, what did happen to you?"

Mary smiled. I explained, and Yvette said, "I'm sorry to hear that. You liked football. That's a shame."

"I did."

"And you've been doing better around the house too. George Rees brought that up in a meeting the other day."

I didn't know the senior residents thought that, so I asked, and from what Yvette told me, they convinced Danny to take me off shot-down, and put me in the kitchen. It would be my first promotion past service crew in six months.

"When are they going to tell me?"

"In the general meeting."

Mary turned to us. "My general meeting."

#

Danny waited for the men to come back from practice, so that he had men to hold Mary down. They beat her for an hour as she cried out in pain. I watched the stranger that stood near the door. He was short, dark, and moved like he was in charge, so I assumed he was staff from Waterford or Parsonsfield. He smiled through the whole thing.

"What the fuck am I going to do with you, Mary Jones? I'm at wits end," Danny said. "I've even brought in a new assistant director to help me out around here because of you." Then he introduced Joe Rodriguez.

Joe started out by telling us that he didn't go through Élan. He had gone through Marathon House, which was the same kind of program. "I'm going to observe for a while before I assume any responsibility."

"That doesn't mean he can't tan your ass if he needs to,"

Danny said, "so don't anyone think they can get out of line."

Then Joe told us his story. They called him 'El Musico' or "The Musician' because he sold heroin out of a violin case. After numerous run-ins with the law, and time in prison, he went to Marathon House to clean up his act. He didn't say how long he had been away from drugs.

"So, you've been to prison, huh?" Danny said. 'Why don't you tell these people a little about their future, because we've got a few prime candidates."

"So, some of you aren't afraid of prison, huh? Well, then you better get ready to suck dick."

He followed by telling us that a tough guy in prison made him suck his dick through the bars, and that before he finished, he bit down as hard as he could. Danny thought that was funny. I crossed my legs. "No one ever messed with me again," Joe said.

Before the meeting ended, Danny did promotions, and I was a member of the kitchen crew. Stan was made my department head and Gary Ross was made my co worker. "Great," he said, "I get to do all the work."

He was referring to my knee. "You get to play football all week, so it ain't all that bad," I said.

"True."

#

Sitting around all day Saturday made me sick because I smoked too much and drank too much coffee. Except for the necessary, I sat in the dining room, and watched everyone. From outside the bubble it was less sane, and more stupid.

The nurse was the first outsider I met in seven months, and I was uneasy around her. She was easy going, and nice to me. It had been so long that it was uncomfortable. I stuttered and couldn't look in her eyes. I was so immersed in Élan's insanity that normal people made me uncomfortable.

Acceptance had gradually made me like them, and after the pressure to confess to being gay was gone, my thing was their thing. I adapted to the yelling and beatings and lack of sleep. Humiliation was assumed. I thought it was pointless until I saw the nurse. It was actually very effective.

Saturday was like any other day, except that free time was longer before and after dinner. That didn't benefit me because I was stuck in one place with my leg up until Monday morning as per the nurse's orders. Sunday brunch had a like effect. It was the same meal I had every day as a football player.

After brunch Danny and Joe had something in the works. The expeditors called fifteen people into the living room, shut them in, and went back to their office. It was a general meeting or haircut/spanking, and it was probably for Mary Jones, so she was agitated and we were apprehensive. Early morning violence would ruin a beautiful day. Eveveryone in the house wanted peace and quiet; everyone that is, but Mary.

I heard the commotion as soon as I woke. Haircuts at the women's dorm were done on the porch, so we got the morning news on who was acting out. It was Mary Jones, Cathy Collins or Donna Fosche, and that morning it was all about Mary. She kept the women up all night, and most of the men.

Danny was quiet; to me he was scariest when he was quiet. With my injuries, I was happy that it wasn't about me. He was flustered that Mary wouldn't conform, that he couldn't see that she was incapable. Not even a masochist could go as far as she did. Instead, he beat her more, which made her act out worse.

Mary was led out of the expeditor's office by Cathy Hogan and Yvette Portella. She smiled at the house when she did, picked up a magazine off the kitchen counter, and tucked it down the back of her shorts. She waved goodbye and laughed. Yvette and Cathy took her into the business office to sit in the corner.

Danny and Joe came out next, and went into the living room. George Rees came out and told the few of us left to sit in the dining room for a general meeting. Then he told Mary to knock on the living room door.

"Who's out there?"

"Mary."

Danny didn't tell her to come in. He opened the door and pulled her into the room and a scuffle broke out. The door was closed and there was a rumble from the room. It sounded like Mary was fighting as they tried to put her over a chair at first, but it didn't stop, and it intensified rather than waned. Everyone in the dining room stared at the living room door in horror as we realized that Mary was getting a cowboy ass kicking.

Mary laughed in the ring, and dealt with the pain of spankings as well as anyone in Élan, but the beating she got in the living room made her scream in agony. I began to cry by the second minute, and wanted Danny Bennison dead by the fifth. When it ended I could barely breathe.

Mary burst out the door, lost her balance, and landed on her stomach. Her face was red and puffy, and her left eye was swollen shut. Her clothes were torn. She pulled her shirt closed, but didn't try to get up.

We thought it was over, but Danny wasn't satisfied. He grabbed Mary by the ankles and dragged her back for five minutes more. When it was over, she was dragged to the front of the dining room. She tried to stand, but couldn't.

"Get up," Danny said.

"I can't."

Danny turned to Joe. "Could you get the paddle from my office?"

"Sure."

When Mary heard, she grabbed the wall and got herself standing. When she did we could see the bruises. They covered half her body. When Joe reentered the dining room with the paddle, she cringed. He looked at her. "So, now will you behave?"

She nodded.

\#

The rest of our Sunday was solemn and quiet. Even the worst residents behaved themselves. It wasn't from fear though—it was in defiance. Danny Bennison spent the day in his office. He left that afternoon without issuing his daily nighttime threats. He didn't need to. There was nothing he could do to top what he did to Mary Jones.

Chapter Nine

The pain from my knee went away after a week but the pain in my shoulder remained. When that went away, I began to hurt myself. I rammed my shoulder against the brick wall in the bathroom and pulled my finger and toe nails off until they bled. It was the only thing that kept me sane. Over the next few weeks I did well and earned privileges.

The football team lost their first game, and Joe Ricci lost his temper. He gave the team a general meeting in Élan Three's dining room and told them their easy days were over. Lunch was cut to fifteen minutes, and was replaced by running laps around the track. He ended by telling them there would be hell to pay if they lost the following week.

Half the men that went out for football were either cut or dropped off the team by the time the season started. Wayne Waver, Allen Kelly and Robert Gamble made the team, but Mike Calabrese, Gary Ross and Matt Brennan didn't. George Rees stayed at the house because he was going home soon, and Dave was too busy to play. We got the daily news from Wayne.

"We did hamburger drills all morning," he said, "And wind sprints all afternoon."

I didn't know what hamburger drills were, but didn't ask. I didn't want to hear about how Mister Know-it-all didn't know everything. Wind sprints were one-hundred-yard dashes from end zone to end zone without breaks in-between. "It's pretty bad," he said.

\#

When the team lost its second game, Joe had a three house general meeting. When we arrived, the team was lined up in front of the room. The crowd yelled as Joe degraded them about their lousy performance then Marty took over.

"Where are the cheerleaders?" he asked. The girls raised their hands. "We won't need you at games any more, but we'll have you drop by practice every morning." He handed Yvette Portella a pad of paper. "These are your new cheers."

"Okay."

"Do you think the girls can give us a preview?"

"Give us ten minutes."

"You have five."

Joe addressed Wayne Barnes while the cheerleaders were in the kitchen going over their routine. "Do you know how hard it was for me to get you on this team?"

Wayne shook his head.

"With the age problem, they wanted you to sit home."

Mike Calabrese told me that Wayne Barnes was twenty years old, and had never finished high school so Joe changed his age to give him an education. It benefitted Joe when the football team was put together, but someone in the school system questioned the age of some of our players, and Joe finagled until he got his way. "Joe always gets his way," he said.

Dominick Parker and Reggie Hammond were next, and then Buddy Guy. They were all from Parsonsfield, so Marty told them how privileged they were to get out of the house at all. They were a tough cast of characters, so I was sure they were all there for murder. Since there were killers in our house that weren't locked up, it was a safe guess.

When the cheerleaders were ready, Marty had them come in the room and do their cheers. They started with Wayne Weaver. "Wayne Weaver really sucks. He plays football like a duck. Let's give him a great big cluck. Quack, quack, quack."

Dave Mogul was next. He had a speech impediment, so the cheer made fun of that. "Mumbley Mogul never talks. Mumbley Mogul always walks. Because he bears a great big cross. Mwah, mwah, mwah."

There was a cheer for each of the first string players, one more degrading than the next, and Marty made the girls perform them all. He ended the meeting by telling the team that they had better not go 0-3 or there would be a new level of hell to pay.

When they lost the following week, I thanked God for my blown out knee.

#

Mary lost her light after the cowboy ass kicking, so the house lost it too. She was one thing that we could interact with that defied the madness we accepted, and though she continued to act out, it was never the same.

Self harm helped me conform. I was given a trip to the big game against Skowhegan. A busload of us was going from all the houses. Everyone wanted to go to the game but Danny picked me and Yvette Portella and I was as surprised as I was happy.

The way to Danny's heart was through his lack of education. He wasn't stupid, and could see that I knew therapy from the years of psychiatric treatment I had received, so he coyly let me lead him in confrontation groups. I was becoming the monster's pet.

\#

Summer school was a series of two hour lectures on subjects that ranged from cooking to outdoor hiking, to life in foreign countries. The subjects were well thought out and interesting so I enjoyed it. Mister Dionne brought in speakers from the outside to tell us about their lives. He had a woman from Italy, and a hippie girl from Jackson Hole, Wyoming.

During a lecture about how to make maple syrup Mister Dionne pointed out the back window, and told us that the cancer crew had cleared away the brush from a dozen maple trees, so for the next two weeks we made pancake syrup.

On Thursday night we had a pep rally for the team, and everyone shouted 'Kill Skowhegan'. Joe Ricci told us that they were the school that tried hardest to keep us from playing with their kids. He called them racists, and burned an Indian in a rowboat on a bonfire twenty feet high. It was fun to pretend, but no one thought we had a chance.

The next night, our boys were beaten by forty-five points and were expecting to be killed by Joe on Sunday, but they weren't. Mike Calabrese told me that he had finally accepted that we didn't belong in the B league football because the teams that we played against had been playing together all their lives and we had thrown a team together in a few months.

"No shit," I said.

\#

That night when the expeditors called a general meeting we thought for sure was for Mary Jones or Donna Fosche, but it wasn't. Danny came out of his office, looked at Cathy Collins, and

67

said "Get up here."

It made sense because Cathy was a problem all day. When Danny called Jane Tolar and Yvette Portella up to join her, I was sure it had to do with the women's group that Mary told me she couldn't talk to me about.

"Then why did you mention it?"

"Because it's big news, Wayne. You're not going to believe it."

"What is it?"

"We'll both get killed if I tell you."

"It's a good thing I don't know about it, then, huh?"

"Yeah."

"You're something, ya know that?"

"Yeah...I know."

Joe Rodriguez came out of the coordinator's office with the gloves and paddle as Wayne Weaver was led out by George Rees and Dave Winston. I was stunned when Yvette and Jane were called to the front of the room, but I was dumbfounded when he came out. Wayne did everything perfectly to avoid confrontation. No one even yelled at him in encounter group. Everyone loved him...except our director.

Danny addressed the house. "So, we had a very enlightening women's group today, and we got to copping to guilt." He looked at Wayne. "And guess whose name came up?"

"I don't know what you're talking about."

"Fuck you, big man. Cathy Collins says otherwise. Get up there with them." He looked back at us. "Seems we have a regular Peyton Place in the coordinator's office. Does anyone have any feeling about this?"

I screamed at Cathy Collins in spite of the fact I had no idea what was going on. Danny would have noticed if I stayed in my seat so I had to scream at someone. He didn't see that she was the only one I yelled at. I called her names and told her that I was tired of her bullshit, and that she better straighten up or she was going to regret it.

I couldn't yell at Wayne, Yvette or Jane, so I sat down when I was done. When we were all seated, Danny continued. "So, Wayne, what are you going to tell me?"

"I'm not going to tell you anything, because I don't have guilt with any of them."

There was no way to not have guilt. If you said that you didn't have any, you were punished for lying. When the topic of guilt came up in the women's group, Cathy Collins said that she had eyes for Wayne Weaver. It wasn't bad guilt to find someone attractive, but according to the program, if you 'have eyes' for someone, you have to say it. All the girls said it about Wayne.

As much as I liked Wayne, he was easy to hate when women were around. One on one, Wayne made you feel big, but when girls were around he made you feel small. It wasn't his fault—it was his nature. Women loved him.

Danny told Cathy Collins to tell her story, and she told us that she gave Wayne Weaver a blowjob in the coordinator's office. I knew she was lying as soon as she said it. The house obviously agreed because they groaned, but Danny went against the sentiment.

"I know you all think Cathy Collins is making this up to stir shit, but she's not the only guilty party, I'm sure, and we're here to figure out who else has been fooling around with our full expeditor."

He started with Jane Tolar. He had the house charge her, then had her spanked until she said that she had given Wayne a blowjob in the coordinators office too. Danny made her tell us about her sex life, and took pleasure in making her say it. From the look on the faces of my fellow residents I wasn't the only one that knew Jane's confession was to make Danny stop beating her.

When Jane had nothing left to take, Danny made degrading remarks about Portuguese women and their fat asses then moved on to Yvette Portella. "I know you've been sucking his cock."

"No, I haven't."

"We'll see about that," he said. "Who wants to go in the ring with her?"

Mary Jones raised her hand.

"Put your hand down, ya fucking nut case. Who's going in the ring with her?"

Yvette was, in her own words 'a tough Puerto Rican', and I saw that she was right when she went five rounds and didn't admit to the lie that Danny wanted. When he showed us the new paddle that Joe Rodriguez made, there was no doubt that she was going to say what he wanted her to say.

It was two inches thick, with ¾ inch holes drilled in it. The only spanking I had given was to Jane Tolar, and that was with hands. The one benefit of being shot down was that I didn't have to abuse anyone. That changed when Danny picked me first.

"C'mon, tough guy. Give her ten."

I had to, so I did. I wanted it to be anyone but her because Yvette made me feel good about myself. She treated me nice. The self abuse that quelled the wide-awake nightmares stopped working when I began spanking her. The flashes of horror started again. Every time the paddle landed, the image of my childhood sweetheart being strangled to death flashed in my head.

"Ten more," Danny said, "and not that limp wristed shit, huh?"

I gave her ten more, and the image flashed ten more times. The nightmare was back in the daylight and I was in a place that tried to beat the nightmares out of you. I sat down when I was done and watched Joe Peterson go next. Then, Pat Carlson and Lisa Kelch went. Yvette lasted to nearly two hundred whacks.

"Okay, okay, I'll tell you," she cried." Just stop."

Danny had two more people go, and then he said, "Go stand next to your boyfriend." When she was standing next to Wayne, he said "Tell us what you did with Wayne."

"We were in the coordinator's office…"

Danny cut her off. "Did you initiate it? I hear you Puerto Rican girls are real feisty."

She knew he wanted her to say it, so she did. "All we ever did is kiss."

"Get the fuck out of here."

"No, seriously, that's as far as it went…Wayne felt me up when we did."

Danny wasn't happy with Yvette's story, so he looked at Willie Garcia and said, "Get up here."

Willie Garcia was gay but he was harmless and funny, so no one gave him a hard time about it. As long as you admitted it, you could live among us and no one cared… except Robert Gamble, of course. Danny picked Robert to go in the ring with Willie, so Willie said he had sex with Wayne as well. It was a lie and everyone knew, but Robert Gamble didn't care. Danny let Robert beat on Willie after the admission for good measure.

For two hours, Wayne wouldn't admit to anything, and it didn't look like that was going to change, so Danny put him in the corner until the van came to take him to Parsonsfield. The girls were all shot down, and I was promoted to department head of the service crew. That brought me one step closer to home.

#

When Wayne Weaver left the house, things went downhill fast. In spite of the consequences, the pressure was too much. Danny threatened us with another tight house, but that didn't work. It was obvious after Mary Jones' cowboy ass kicking that the house had animosity for Danny, but when he made Willie Garcia say that he had sex with Wayne, he crossed a line he shouldn't have. Mary Jones said "Cathy Collins and Willie Garcia are full of shit. Wayne didn't let those two touch him."

No one corrected her. Danny heard her and said nothing. Instead, he picked up a clipboard and left the room. He talked about psychic vampires, said they were people who sucked your emotions. After Wayne's general meeting I knew what he was talking about. Danny had left us nothing. He had bled me of every emotion but hate.

Chapter Ten

When Danny Bennison didn't come to work for a few days, people began to wonder where he was, but by the end of two weeks we were sure he wasn't coming back. Joe Rodriguez became our new director by default. No one ever announced why Danny was gone but we knew it was because of what he did to Mary Jones. The word was that Joe Ricci found out that Mary was given a cowboy ass kicking and removed Danny from the house.

"They have him at another house. I saw him the other day."

"They should get rid of that motherfucker, Mike."

"Amen," Gary Ross agreed.

Joe was better than Danny in one respect. He just wanted peace. Danny tore at people to satisfy his convoluted ideas of why they were drug users More times than not he blamed homosexuality. In some of those cases he may have been right, but most of the time he was wrong.

"Do you think Wayne Weaver let Willie Garcia blow him?" I asked Mike and Gary one day.

They laughed, and Mike said "No one believed that bullshit, dude. Did you?"

"No."

"That was Danny being Danny."

"What about Cathy Collins?" I asked.

"No way he let that skank touch him either," Gary answered.

When I asked about Jane and Yvette they both said that they were on the fence. "I'm almost sure about Yvette," Mike said, "but Jane I don't know about."

Gary nodded.

#

Joe was heavy-handed but he only beat on people who acted out. I had found a razor blade in the service crew office and cut myself, so I did well. Self mutilation was tricky in close quarters but I was good at hiding it. People even began to like me when I took over the Shot Pulling Newspaper.

The Shot Pulling Newspaper was supposed to be therapeutic, but no one ever explained how. It was done by someone who was doing well, and under Joe I did well. The previous shot-pullers were sarcastic, which was funny to everyone but the person the jokes were about. After a while everyone had gotten a dose of it and didn't like the shot puller very much.

The objective was to target a person's character defects or image. Mister Cool and Mister Know-it-all were popular. there were lots of jokes about who had eyes for who, who was getting too close to a member of the opposite sex. I did jokes with songs and slogans, making it funny. The people in the house looked forward to it every morning. Joe Rodriguez found out and came to listen.

\#

Everyone loves you when you're on top. I was picked to go on trips to town to see movies and go shopping. I was chosen by Miss Libby to attend a special class where she planned to teach us table manners. The payoff was a trip to the restaurant -- No Tomatoes, a fancy place in town. It was a great meal. I took the class just to be around Miss Libby.

"She's a real piece of ass," Mike Calabrese said.

"Keep it clean with Miss Libby," Gary Ross warned. "She's my favorite teacher."

"Same here," I said. "Her and Miss Russell."

Mike smiled. "Now, Miss Russell...she's a piece of ass."

"Yeah," Gary agreed. "Miss Russell is a piece of ass."

"You guys don't get women, do you?" I replied.

"Why don't you explain it to us, Mister Know-it-all?"

"Hey! fuck you, Mike."

He laughed, then shrugged. "What do you mean, we don't get women?"

"That shit is degrading to women."

They laughed, and when I tried to speak they laughed harder. "Keep it up guys. Girls don't like guys that talk like that about them, and I don't know how they know, but they do. All the guys in my father's bar that talked like that never had girlfriends."

Gary and Mike stopped laughing, so I finished. "Girls like guys that treat them nice. Shit, look at Wayne Weaver. He ain't

that good looking…He's a gentleman. The cool girls all like him."
They agreed.

"Y'know what, don't take my advice, but do me a favor; don't talk that way about Miss Russell. She was nice to me once"

As we finished our cigarettes, Mike told us about a girl he liked that had an asshole boyfriend like that. Gary had a story too. I didn't, but made one up to seem normal. Mike and Gary weren't just my goofball friends. We shared feelings as well as guilt. Still, I couldn't tell them the truth about me.

\#

On Christmas day we got candy. It was supposed to be a treat but by the time we got it, the staff had threatened to take it away so many times that I didn't care. I didn't enjoy it at all. The part of me that attached itself to things had gone, and had begun to attach itself to people. Christmas saw a lot of people leave.

Denise, George and Dave went first, then Allen Kelly and Robert Gamble. Cathy Hogan followed. I celebrated when Robert left, but the rest took little pieces of me with them, like guys going home from the war. Even Denise wasn't so bad if you looked in her eyes when you talked to her.

Denise didn't know psychology, but she knew people. In the last group she ran, she told me that she never believed Matt Brennan, and that she told that to Danny. When she said she liked me I was surprised. "Thank you."

"I also think there's something seriously wrong with you, that this place is never going to hear about."

I looked directly at her tits, but she didn't care. She asked, "Why haven't you ever copped to having eyes for anyone?"

She noticed, so I was trapped. I told her that I had eyes for all of the black and Puerto Rican women in the house. Where I came from that made me a race traitor, so I grew up thinking there was something wrong with me. According to the guys in my father's bar it was okay to have sex with a black woman, but it was a sin against God to love one.

"My first girlfriend was Puerto Rican…her name was Maria."

Yvette snapped her fingers. "Hey, Wayne's a ladies' man."

Everyone laughed, so I looked away.

"Hey," she said, "I'm serious."

"What do you mean?"

"Girls like you, is what I'm saying."

I smiled. "Maria told me that I was handsome, and rugged, like John Wayne, but no one's said it since."

"Really?" Denise said.

I told her that women didn't like me, but Denise disagreed, and over the next twenty minutes I found out that everything I thought women hated about me, they liked. Then Denise asked me how I felt about my looks, and I told her one of my secrets.

"I shave without a mirror."

"What?"

"I haven't looked into a mirror since I was ten. The last time I did, I filled my mouth with water and spit it into an electric socket."

"Whoa, you mean, you tried to kill yourself?"

"I was thrown across the room."

"Why?"

"My face was so ugly, I wanted to die."

"Dude, you're beautiful," Denise said. "Ask anyone in this group."

I was teased about my looks all my life so I didn't know what to believe. "Are you serious?"

They nodded.

I was happy the group ended because I couldn't tell everything. Denise was right about the fact that Élan was never going to hear my darkest secrets. I saw what they did with people's secrets.

\#

Because of the lack of coordinators in the house Joe brought in assistant directors, Diane Hozman, Neal Kurzman, and Jeanine Dubrielle. They went through the program at Élan Three and were going to run the therapy part of the house schedule as Joe took care of the discipline. Joe was good at that.

Before they arrived Joe had made Yvette the coordinator of the cleaning crew and me the department head, so I gave haircuts, ran groups, and did night man duty. I had no idea what I was doing and was happy when they came in.

Mike Calabrese was promoted to the service crew. Nine months after being my boss he was my worker. The dichotomy changed a lot. Cathy Hogan was once promoted from shot-down to full coordinator at a meeting, so people that were screaming in her face the day before were working for her in the blink of an eye.

That night Neil said to me "Take Mike Calabrese down to the dorm, and take over as night man when the house gets there."

The house was finishing nighttime snacks, so I put mine on the night man's tray and Mike grabbed the cleaning equipment. We walked down the path to the dorm."There's going to be an inspection tomorrow. So whatever you can do tonight to save yourself time tomorrow would be smart."

"I know what to do, Wayne. I've been through this a few times before."

"Yeah, well, make it good. I don't wanna catch hell from Yvette."

We climbed the stairs, crossed the porch, and opened the door. When I turned on the light, a man was standing there.

\#

I beat Mike to the house by two steps. I had never seen him move so fast. When we got to the door, the house was gathered in the dining room in their coats waiting to go to the dorms. When we crashed through the door they knew we were afraid.

Neil said, "What the hell happened to you two?"

"There was someone in the dorm."

"What do you mean?"

Mike told the story, and finished with, "I threw the cleaning stuff in the air, and Wayne's night tray went over the side of the porch."

"That was the pervert," Mary Jones said. "He used to come around here all the time when I was first here."

Neil shook his head. "What are you talking about? I've never heard of a pervert."

"It was before you got here. Remember Magna Vera? She walked in on the pervert in the girl's dorm once, when Alan Frey was the director."

"Those are just ghost stories," Neil said. "They were made up to scare people, so they wouldn't run away at night."

"No they're not."

\#

Over the next week there were four more pervert sightings. Everyone was afraid, so I wasn't sure if any of them were real, but it didn't matter. Everyone was afraid. We had guys from Élan Three come down to the dorms as extra security at night. That's when I ran into Mike Skakel again.

He stopped to talk to me. "Hey, man, what's going on? You look like you're doing good."

"I am doing good. How are you?"

"I'm hanging in there. What's this all about?"

"The pervert."

"What pervert?"

I explained what happened, and Mike laughed. He started telling me that there was no such thing as the pervert when we heard the girls scream. "It's the pervert!"

"Get the fuck out of here," Mike said, and started towards the dorm.

An hour later, Joe Ricci called a general meeting at our house.
#
I had only seen Joe in passing, but from what I saw, I didn't want a close relationship. He dressed like a pimp, acted like he was black and Mike Calabrese told me he was in the mafia.

He waited until everyone was seated. It was quick and quiet. The big boss could have you disappear, so he got our best behavior. "I'm going to say this once," he said, "and then, we're never going to mention it again. There is no pervert, there never was a pervert, and no one has ever seen him. Do we have that straight?"

"Yes," we said.

"Good, because I'm tired of this bullshit." He lit a cigarette. "This house is the worst of the bunch and I'm tired of hearing about it."

He went on for ten minutes about Mary Jones and Donna Fosche, and then told us that he wanted to see a significant change in our house. "I don't mean in a year, or a month, or a day," he said, "I mean immediately."

He put out his cigarette and Diane took over the meeting. "Wayne Kernochan and Mike Calabrese, you two started this, so you're both shot down."

She continued but I stopped listening. One of the slogans that people slung around was that 'the world is full of injustices; get used to it'. I hated that slogan before I was shot down. "Show up in shorts and a tee shirt tomorrow morning, and scrub the kitchen floor all day," Diane said.

When Diane was done, Joe said, "Good night," and left, then we went to the dorms, to bed, and no one ever saw the pervert again. Mike Calabrese told me that Joe had him shot and killed, and though that sounded outrageous, I didn't completely doubt it.

#

The next morning was my worst in the program. As a shot-down, I was watched all the time, so I couldn't cut myself, and the nightmares came back. To make it worse, Diane blamed all that I did wrong on the fact that I was such a clown. The thing people loved about me was turned against me again. I was in a clown suit by spring.

Kelly Clapp sat me down the first morning. That was the day I had my first sexual thought. Except for Maria, I had never been touched by a girl, but when Kelly's finger touched my face it was obvious that I liked girls.

One of my secrets was that I didn't know if I was gay or straight, because I had never had a sexual thought before then. The deeper part of it was that I thought I was a serial killer. As I got older, as I began to get aroused by violence rather than sex, I knew there was something wrong with me. It was somehow lost in the dreams and flashes, that had started in a basement in East New York, Brooklyn.

Chapter Eleven

Kernochan's Bar and Grill stood on the corner of Cleveland and Fulton Streets in East New York, Brooklyn for decades. My grandmother and grandfather opened the place and it thrived for many years. Grandpa died when I was young so I didn't remember him.

My grandmother, who I called Nana, was my father's partner. She was a tough lady and I loved her. She was good for a hundred dollars on an occasion, and if you stopped by the bar at night after she had a few, she would let you grab as much change from her change dish as your hand could hold. But it wasn't just the money that attracted you to my grandmother, it was her personality. She didn't take shit from anyone.

My Nana once knocked a guy off his stool and on his ass in the family restaurant for making my brother cry. She wasn't a caricature—she really was tough. Matilda Kernochan sat on her stool at the end of the bar and railed the drunks mercilessly. When someone ordered a simple beer, she was known to comment. "Beers are chasers for whatever a real man drinks."

I laughed.

Once, as I walked down ClevÉland Street to the bar, the kids on the block started messing with me. There were six or seven of them and I was alone so it was a losing proposition to fight. There was a neighborhood song for situations when someone fights a guy on your block. "A fight, a fight, a nigger and a white, if the white don't win, we all jump in." This didn't just apply to nigger; it applied to your relationships with the whites. Sometimes you become the nigger. All I knew was that I should take the verbal barbs and keep walking.

"Look at the little faggot," The big one said, daring me to say a word.

"He walks like he just got fucked in the ass," another said.

79

"Yeah, he definitely is a faggot. Do you suck dick, faggot?" someone shouted.

I kept walking, ready to break into a run if I needed to, as tears came to my eyes. It wasn't just their words that bothered me, it was the fact that I was cowering out of a fight. I pushed my hands down as far into my pockets as I could and stared down the block to the bar to see if there was someone there who could take my back. I wanted to punch that big guy in the face and take the subsequent beating just to show him and his pals that I wasn't afraid of any of them in a fair fight.

Every kid in my neighborhood wanted to be a tough guy, but they called me Face. It became my nickname because my older brother and his friends would take turns punching me in the face. It hurt, but I took it without a whimper. I wasn't afraid of a beating.

But there I was crying like a girl as I got to the bar, and Nana must have seen it or heard what happened because she handed me a baseball bat that my parents brought back from a trip to Spain and said "Go back up there and stand up for yourself, or you're out of my will."

They were gone when I went back or I might have killed someone.

#

As for our neighborhood, it was divided into blocks. If we were the same color, we all pretty much got along with each other, but in sports, for the sake of territory it was your block against the other block. We played stickball and roller hockey and basketball. The best were the games made up or exaggerated from other games like hide and seek or tag. Our parents didn't let us sit around the house doing nothing, and in those days TV was off limits.

"Get out and stay out until dinner," my mother would say. Mom was a beautiful woman. Everyone agreed, so I assumed it was true. What no one told me was that Mom had a secret. She had eight kids, so she wasn't so much interested in us being social as she was in getting us out of the house to have quality alone-time to drink.

Mom was also strange because sometimes she would change everything about herself, her hair, face and nails, and she would wear wigs that she kept on Styrofoam heads in her bedroom. She would transform herself into a starlet—she certainly was beautiful then. She looked like a movie star at an opening. "Your mom looks like Gloria Swanson," Uncle Mike used to say.

Gloria Swanson was a movie actress, and though I'd never seen her movies I was sure that she was great. I fantasized that Mom actually was Gloria Swanson. When my father and she dressed up to go out, she was the guest of honor.

As soon as they left and the babysitter was busy with other things, I would go into my parent's room and pretend I was at the party. The Styrofoam heads were guests and we were there to give out an Academy Award. I was on the A-list of course. Dad wasn't, but Mom was. She was my mother, and all movie stars attended events with their mother. Of course, I was a movie star too.

I was a well known actor and the ex-husband of Marilyn Monroe, and people were always happy to see me. We drank cocktails from oddly-shaped glasses and laughed like the guys in the bar—loud and boisterous.

The styro-head with the wig was mom, talking about her favorite film to the masses. The other was bareheaded—because mom wore that wig when she went out—so though it was white, it was a bald black woman with a long neck, strong and sexy, like a character from a James Bond movie. She had crew-cut-length hair that she described as, "suede eight-ball," in her deep sultry voice.

She was my date.

The party lasted until my parents came home or the babysitter shooed me off to bed, and real life came back to haunt again. I liked my fantasy world very much. Real life, real friends and family were what I hated. It was all too strange for me.

\#

The main entrance of Highland Park was red brick with tall black wrought iron fencing. There was a playground on the right and a basketball court on the left. I played hockey with my brothers and friends on the basketball court, but when I was alone I liked to hang out in the playground near the grown-up swings and pretend I was pushing the beautiful girls like lovers did in movies.

As I turned right into the playground that day I stopped. She had the face of an angel. I tried to move but couldn't for a second, then control of my body came back just in time to make me look awkward. I looked away from her for a minute, and eventually my brain came back to me. It arrived just in time for the trembling and shaking—something girls love in a man.

I righted myself and looked away so that she wouldn't catch me staring. It was uncomfortable to look in her direction for very long, but from my short clandestine looks I was convinced she was the most beautiful girl in the world. I imagined that she was Maria and I was Tony, in West Side Story, and we were in the park enjoying our time away from the violence and the hate, and the people who say they love you but don't.

Her hair was straight and shiny-black. When she moved it swayed and sparkled in the sun. It hung down to her waist and she was tall like me, with dark coffee colored skin. She was every bit as beautiful as Natalie Wood, and was sitting just two feet away from me. Then she threw her head back and hit me in the face with her hair.

Whoosh—it smelled like perfume.

She jumped off the swing. "Oh my God, I'm sorry!"

It felt like she had caught me looking up her dress. The look on my face certainly gave away the fact I was stalking her. I smiled, trying to look confused. "Wow, you have the longest hair I've ever seen."

The pride she took in her hair was obvious when she smiled back at me. "Yeah, but it looks horrible in this wind."

"No, it doesn't," I said. "It's beautiful. I wish my parents would let me grow my hair that long."

"Long hair looks silly on a boy."

I felt silly because I'd always wanted long hair, like a rock star.

"I don't think David Cassidy looks silly."

"It looks good for him because he's on TV."

"I'm going to be on TV some day."

"You?"

I looked at her seriously, "Yes me, like my mother. She's better than Gloria Swanson."

It must have been a convincing lie, because she looked impressed.

"You're going to be a movie star? That sounds wonderful."

I held out my hand. "I'm Wayne."

"Pleased to meet you, Wayne. I'm Maria."

She was Maria. Boy, did I wish my name was Tony, or

anything but Wayne. I told her how much I hated my name. "I like your name; you're like John Wayne, a big strong man," Maria said. "I like strong men like John Wayne."

I loved the idea that she thought I was tough, but John Wayne was a little intimidating for a twelve-year-old to live up to, so I laughed. "That's me, my brother's name is John and I'm Wayne. We're John Wayne."

She wasn't wearing a uniform from a Catholic school, so I assumed she went to the public school. She looked beautiful in her jeans and Tee-shirt though. We sat on the grown-up swings and life was nice for an hour, but then I had to go.

"I need to go to work," I said. "You can go with me if you want."

"Sure," she said. "I'd like that."

I was in love.

\#

My job was an entrepreneurial venture for a twelve-year-old kid. There was a recycling place on Atlantic Avenue that paid a penny a pound for old newspapers. I didn't know why they would want old newspapers, but I knew where to get my hands on thousands of them behind the apartment buildings on Jamaica Avenue.

Usually I collected with a friend from school, like Mike Abbondanza or Billy Billotto, but that changed when I met Maria. We met after school and on weekend days in the morning near the entrance to the park to go to work. I had to keep her a secret from my brothers and friends because they would have teased me mercilessly. I could hear it in my head: "Wayne has a girlfriend, ha-ha!"

To avoid the shame we didn't go around the block. Besides, she was Puerto Rican and the guys in the neighborhood didn't like Puerto Ricans very much. They called them spics and savages.

It was unusually hot that day so we stopped for a soda. "I'm going to have a Wink." I said. Mom drank Wink, so it was movie star soda, and it was all I ever drank -- at least that was my story. "My mother drinks Wink."

"It's sour," Maria said, and grimaced.

"You develop a taste for it." I didn't know what that meant, but it sounded good when someone in the bar said it.

"I don't think I'll do that. I don't like sour things." She pulled a strange colored can out of the fridge and showed me the label, "I like sweet sodas." She pulled it back and popped open a Champagne Cola.

I couldn't find any Wink, and said it loud enough, then settled on a Champagne Cola myself. "I've had this before." I said.

She held the door for me. "Sure you have."

"No, really, my friend Carlos drinks this."

"Really?"

Carlos was crazy, but he told great stories, so we kids would hang out with him and his dog, King, in the park. I told Maria about Carlos, and she knew him.

"I love King, he's so beautiful," she said.

"King bit me."

"King bit you?"

"My foot, he bit my foot once."

"You must have scared him," she said.

"That must have been it."

We filled the cart and I rolled it down Linwood Street by myself, as Maria waited by the bushes on the corner. When I got back, the subject of race came up. "Why can't I go on your block? Are you ashamed of me?"

I explained to her that people who had never met her hated her because of her nationality. I didn't really understand it myself, and I let her know that I wasn't like that. "I really, really, like you Maria. I don't hate anyone."

"You do?"

"Yes, I do."

She put on a playful face and asked "How much do you really, really like me?"

"A lot… I like you a lot. I think I love you."

The facetious look gave way to a softness that made me want to kiss her, but I chickened out—she might pull away, and then what? Instead I took her hand like a knight takes the hand of a princess, and I kissed it.

Maria closed her eyes and smiled, but then she grabbed my hand hard and pulled me to her. "My father hates white people…he would kill me if he saw us together."

"So we're like Tony and Maria in West Side Story," I said.

She hadn't seen the movie, so I told her the story of love and hate, and the inevitable violence. "That's a terrible story," Maria said. "I don't like sad endings."

"Me neither."

There was a wrought iron ladder with black metal steps leading down to where the garbage cans were at our next stop that day. It was a courtyard, and it looked forbidding. There were bails of paper tied up and ready for the taking, but we looked at each other and her eyes spoke to me: 'It's wrong to go down there.'

I was a tough guy, like John Wayne, so I wasn't scared. I shrugged and went down the ladder. She fell in behind, just a few rungs above me. When we were both safely on the ground she grabbed my shoulder and there was a flash.

That's when the nightmares began.

Chapter Twelve

Monsters don't look like monsters. I know because I've met them in my dreams and my dreams are real. Maria stopped coming to meet me one day and I couldn't remember why until the nightmares began.

Monsters are sweaty, angry human creatures that spit when they speak and laugh at pain. I know because I met them in a basement in Brooklyn. The problem is that my dreams didn't reveal enough to know what really happened. I didn't know what to say or who to say it to, so I kept it to myself. By the time I got to Élan, I knew what happened in that basement, but the truth was blurred by the pain and anxiety of my life. By then they would have blamed me.

If I didn't sleep I couldn't dream, so I kept myself up for days. When I was young my parents thought I was an insomniac, but I stayed on my feet to keep awake in my room at night to avoid the nightmares. I lasted eleven days once.

Cutting was easier than denying myself sleep, so when I didn't need a personal overseer in the bathroom I cut myself, and the nightmares went away. In short time I was off shot-down and back on the service crew. By the time they brought in Michael Blackman I was a department head again.

Michael was perfectly normal when he came to Élan, but after a few months in the program he had a nervous breakdown and was the talk of Poland Springs. His behavior was outrageous. Joe Rodriguez pointed to his head and said "He's scrambled eggs."

The powers-that-be decided that he was faking insanity to get out of the program and that they were going to unscramble his eggs with beatings. We were called to a three house general meeting for him one day, which Peter McCann started off with a comedy routine.

Mike had a pasta pot over his head as he stood in front of the house, and when everyone was seated, Peter took a serving spoon and banged it against the side as hard as he could. Then he looked at the pot, and asked, "S'alright?"

He pulled the pot off his head, and Mike said, "S'alright."

He put the pot back on, and banged it again, then stopped, and said, "S'okay?"

He took it off again. "S'okay."

He repeated it with different words, as Joe, Peter and the lower staff laughed. Between the ring and the paddle they accused Mike of faking mental illness to get out of Élan. Joe let him know that it wasn't going to work. "We'll do this forever," he said.

And on it went.

\#

By fall, Mike had been to our house three times to be beaten and humiliated, but the guys in our house went easy on him. By that time, he had the boxing gloves duct taped to his wrists because he was hurting himself. It was clear that he wasn't faking.

It was months before they gave up on Michael Blackman. One day, Mike Calabrese told me that he was gone, and no one was allowed to talk about it. I was sad to see him go because there was a kinship between us. We were two of the very few people that didn't give Élan what they wanted in spite of the consequences. Mary Jones felt it too. "I'm gonna miss him," she said.

My coordinator was Yvette Portella, so the promotion to department head had perks. Yvette was as easy to work for as she was to look at. "You've had this job before, right? she said. "So, you know what you're doing."

"Yeah, I do."

"So, what do we do now?"

We had an hour for orientation and were done in two minutes. I suggested that we go out on the porch so that I could cop to my guilt. She got her notebook and pen and we went outside. "So, what kind of guilt do you have to cop to?" she asked.

"This is kind of a tough one," I said, "because, it's about guilt I already copped to."

"What do you mean?"

I told her that when Danny was running the house I copped to something that wasn't real because Danny pressured me to. I told her that I wasn't lying about the situation with Matt Brennan, but that Danny wanted something, so I told him lies about Kip Neville to appease him.

Yvette put her pen down and closed the notebook. "You can't do this."

"Why not?"

"Wayne," she said, "what's in the past, stays in the past. Nobody wants to go back there."

"But, it's true, and it's my guilt."

"It's mine too, y'know, but it's over and done with. Dude, I'm advising you to keep this shit to yourself." Then she looked around, to be sure we were having a private conversation. "You know that I never messed around with Wayne Weaver, right?"

"I was always sure of it."

"Neither did Jane, or Cathy, or Willie Garcia," She looked around again. "I mean, c'mon. Willie Garcia for Christ's sake!"

"Can't you help Wayne by telling the truth?"

"No. They're never going to admit that Danny was wrong, so shut your mouth."

"That's fucked up."

"I know it is," she said, "but I'm going home soon, and I ain't fucking that up now. I'm getting out of this place, and you should too."

"I guess."

Yvette and I then had a contract, so I finished with more guilt than when we started, but that would have to wait until she was gone. I wasn't going to get in the way of her getting out, but I wasn't going to let it go. I was playing a dangerous game by bad rapping the program, but the ubiquitous hatred for Danny Bennison was strong enough to get away with it if I played my cards right. Wayne deserved that. We all did.

Chapter Thirteen

After more than a year in the program I had been shot down more than half the time, but when Joe and Diane were directors I did better. Diane yelled a lot but she wasn't violent, so I liked her. At sixteen months I escaped the insanity again by signing up for football. It was especially inviting that year because Neal Kurzman hated me and looked for reasons to bust my balls so I needed to get away from the house.

When I was new, he was 'Neal the Eel' and he slithered around because of the way he felt. Nothing changed but his facial hair, so I was happy to get away from Neal the Eel. The psychic vampires were too much for people like me. I preferred a punch in the nose over the conniving ways some people got others to do it for them. Neal was like that.

Élan had softened, so we were pretty sure that football was going to be less severe. By then Joe said that he figured out our problem and that it was unfixable. We stunk. Most of the good players from the first season were gone by the second so it looked like we were going to match the previous year's record of 0-8 so the pressure was off. I signed up, and swore I would follow it through that year no matter what kind of injury.

"I'll be the wheelchair water boy if I have to," I said to Shane McGarrah.

"You'll be that if they put you against me," Gary Ross said.

"Dude, you're both on defense," Shane said.

\#

We met in the morning for a feast of real eggs, pancakes and three different kinds of meat, and we drank as much coffee as we wanted. I knew who was going to make the team and who wasn't immediately. For some it was going to be their only football meal. At one point, Joe Peterson looked at Bill Miller and Ben Grimes, shook his head and laughed.

When breakfast was done we met our teammates from Élan

Three, and the first face I recognized was Michael Skakel. He spoke first "I see you're doing good again."

"It was inevitable," I said.

He laughed. "Well, keep it up, huh?"

"I hope to. I can't wait to get out of here."

"Me neither."

#

The men from Parsonsfield and Waterford were brought by bus, which was arriving as we got to the main parking lot. "We go everywhere as a team," Marty Kruglick said, "and anyone that wanders off by themselves is cut."

The next familiar face I saw was Wayne Weaver. He looked older. His face was sad and his spirit was broken, I could tell. He saw me and nodded. Then he smiled. "Hey there, man, how are you doing?"

"I'm pretty good, pal. I'm department head of the service crew. How about you?"

"I'm shot down," he said, and told me that his time at Parsonsfield wasn't going well. Danny had turned everyone against him so he was always in trouble. I thought about telling him what Yvette had told me, but she was scheduled to go home the next day.

"You better get your shit together, Dude. You were my favorite expeditor."

He laughed. "That was a long time ago."

"It sure was...A lifetime."

Marty interrupted us. "Gentlemen, I want a straight line, and I want you all with your houses. I want constant headcounts." He turned to Jamie Newfield. "You're senior expeditor, so I want the senior from each house to report to you."

Jamie nodded.

Then Marty looked at us. "If there's a repeat of last year's split, there's going to be hell to pay."

The previous year, two players took off from football practice and had been taken to every house for a general meeting. Then they were taken to the practice field for a football team general meeting where they were subjected to hamburger drills for hours.

In a hamburger drill you stood in one place, and the team lined up and hit you one by one. It was designed to teach you to avoid a hit but after enough time you became too weak to get out of the way. Every hit slowed you down more, so eventually you were helpless.

I wasn't going anywhere.

#

The practice field was long and grassy. The spring dew glistened in the early morning sun. We were ready to play football. The tackling dummies and blocking sleds were neatly lined up at the far end of the field near the end zone against the trees. They had been purposely pushed off to the side.

Joe Peterson turned to me. "Looks like we're going to be doing a lot of running today."

I agreed, and thought about my bad knee. "I hope we do calisthenics. My knee won't take too much of that."

"Then, you better hope."

I changed the subject. "Did you see Wayne Weaver?"

"Yeah, I did," he said, "But I was kind of new when he left, so I didn't say anything to him."

"He's shot down."

"Wasn't he a coordinator when he got shot down?"

"Full expeditor...The best," I said, "Till that G.M."

He didn't say anything. Neither did I.

#

We ran laps and did calisthenics before lunch and played soccer when we were done eating. Marty gave us a two-hour lunch break so that the people in positions could give haircuts to their housemates. The rest of us kicked the ball around.

Mike Skakel and I ended up on the same team, and we won by seven goals. When it was over, we sat under the trees at the end of the field and smoked a cigarette. "I see Wayne Weaver is here," he said. "Have you talked to him?"

"Yeah,"

"And?"

"And, what?" I said. "He's miserable over there."

"Between you and me, Danny was a scumbag for sending him there."

"What kind of threat does he pose because of that bullshit anyway?" I said.

"I guess he poses a danger to loose women."

I laughed dryly. "But, those confessions were bullshit, y'know that?"

"Yeah…I know."

"I guess you're going to tell him to admit it and get it over with."

"Nah," he said. "This place is changing. I'm not going to do anything of the sort."

I stubbed out my cigarette. "Just so we're even…Between you and me, Yvette Portella already admitted to me that she lied."

"Then why don't you tell someone?"

"When she's gone tomorrow, I'll talk to him about it."

"You better. The guy is suffering."

#

When practice was over I said goodbye to Wayne, then we walked the Élan Three guys to their house. Joe Peterson led us down the hill. I was tired and my muscles hurt. The first day was always bad, and I knew it would be worse by morning.

"Thank God I'm on the bottom bunk," I said.

"Same here," Joe said, "unlike McGarrah here."

Shane McGarrah was newer than Joe and I, so he was still on a top bunk. The season before, the main complaint at the beginning of practice was having a top bunk. Mike Calabrese tore a muscle in his leg getting out of bed.

"I'm going to ask Marty to get me a bottom bunk," Shane said.

"Good luck with that," Joe said. "We have expeditors sleeping on top bunks as it is. There's no room on the bottom."

"I'm gonna ask anyway. What could it hurt?"

"Go ahead."

As we walked in the front door, there was a general meeting going on. Donna Fosche was standing in front of the room, and Diane was talking to her. Danny and Joe never talked to someone after a G.M.—they beat them and left. It was the reason I liked Diane.

Donna was becoming boring. Every few days she would cause a commotion and if the staff ignored it she would go berserk. She was alert and normal one minute, and then, in a few seconds it was obvious that she belonged with Michael Blackman in a hospital. Donna wasn't crazy all the time, but she was crazy. I knew because

I was crazy. She knew about me too, so every once in a while she would look at me and shake her head. "They just don't get it."

"No, they don't."

Diane was in the middle of the speech that they always used on Donna, about her seeking attention, so I stopped paying attention right away. I was checking out Jeff Gottlieb. I knew him from a general meeting but had never seen him in our house.

Diane paused for a few seconds, and Jeffrey stepped in. "So, what is it you want Donna?" He pronounced her name with a thick Boston accent, so it came out Dawna.

"Nothing."

"Nothing?" He lit a cigarette.

"Nothing," she said.

"So, then, the answer is nothing."

Donna looked confused. She wasn't alone. The house was already wondering why Jeff was there, but got edgy when he started to speak. The rumor about him was that he locked a girl and a gay kid in a room with two rapists and let them do what they wanted. I didn't believe it, but some people did.

He turned to us. "From now on, Donna does nothing, smoking, coffee, activities, school, all of it. She sits right over there," He pointed to the table in the corner, "and she does nothing." He turned to her. "How does that sound?"

"Fine," she said.

He took Donna by the elbow and led her to her table. "Now, that's where you stay until you're ready to join the rest of the house."

Diane addressed the house. "For those of you that don't know, this is Jeffrey Gottlieb. He's going to be your new director.

93

Chapter Fourteen

Monday morning brought dark skies and the threat of rain, but our first practice scrimmage was close, so Marty insisted that the football team meet in Élan Three's dining room to be sure of the weather. When we arrived, the players from Three were huddled around tables talking. We waved to the ones we knew.

Mike Skakel was with Jamie Newfield and John Higgins. He nodded to me when we arrived. Joe Peterson liked to be in charge so I let him pick our table and situate the guys. He did it in a loud, military manner.

"You guys stay here and behave yourselves," Marty said, "and I'll go get the guys from the bus."

Only Shane McGarrah was lower than Joe, Gary and I, and Joe needed to look like the boss so he looked at Shane. "Did you hear what he said? Behave yourself until he gets back."

Shane said "I heard him."

"Did I tell you to cop an attitude?"

There was no right answer to that question so Shane didn't say anything, but that wasn't enough for Joe. He was in his first position of authority and it was obvious that he enjoyed it. He would have fit in perfectly in the old days. "You're not denying it, so now I'm sure you were copping an attitude," he said.

"I wasn't."

"Now you're lying." Joe asked Jamie Newfield "Is there a room I can use?"

Jamie pointed.

Joe said to Shane. "Knock on this door."

Shane muttered something about Joe being on a power trip as he passed me and I would have said something, but I agreed. We didn't nitpick at football. The guys from Three were also uncomfortable because of it.

When Joe was done, Marty and the players arrived. The commotion drowned out Joe's victory lap, and Shane chose to blend in rather than take the walk through a tense, quiet dining room. Wayne Weaver was having a conversation with one of the guys from his house. When he saw me I gestured to him that we needed to talk, and he nodded. He put his hand to his face and mimicked eating a sandwich to tell me that we should do it at lunchtime. I nodded.

#

"Jane Tolar told me that she's going to tell Jeffrey that she lied on you, man."

"Really?"

I told him the story from the beginning and he looked happy at first, but by the time I was done he looked angry again. Yvette and Jane were a small victory compared to Cathy Collins and Willie Garcia.

"I'm working on Willie and Cathy, but if Jeff gets mad at Jane and tells us to stop talking about the old days, I'll never be able to confront them."

"Then tell her to shut up about it for a while."

"She spoke to him last night. She might have already told him."

#

That night, I had my first coordinator's meeting with Jeff Gottlieb and Gary Ross. Jeff started by telling us that Jane had been shot down for guilt that she had copped to, and then he made me the chief coordinator, Joe Peterson a coordinator, and Gary the coordinator of the department heads.

I cut myself for fun and I was in charge of the house. Twenty-five people's lives were in the hands of a fifteen-year-old who wanted to kill someone. After the next week's scrimmage game we were scheduled to start the season. Summer was coming to an end and so was my time away from the house. Before long they were going to figure me out.

Jane congratulated me on the promotion. "You'll be going home soon," she said. "I'll miss you."

"I'm not out of here yet."

"You're doing good. You'll be out of here soon."

#

If someone makes you angry and you want to sit on the end of your chair in an encounter group screaming at them, you 'drop a slip' on them. Encounter groups took precedent over other groups, so there were a lot more of them. There were rarely slips in the box for static groups.

As the participants set up to scream, they'd let you know who they were angry at. When it began three or four people would start yelling at the same time. Usually one outlasted the other. In the event that two or more people were going on for too long the group leader had to assign an order.

Cathy Collins yelled at Jane Tolar for getting shot down because she considered her a role model. When she was done Gary asked me to be in charge of the group for as long as it took for him to yell at Jane too. Jane didn't shout at them, which was rare for her. She was dejected and embarrassed, so she sat and took it.

When Gary was done, he said, "One more," and went after Cathy Collins for having the nerve to yell at Jane. Cathy called him corrupt and said he had no right to yell at her. The language had changed in the year and half I was in Élan, but it was easy to see that the residents still hated and wanted to hurt each other.

When the yelling was over Gary confronted Jane about losing her job and asked her what guilt she had copped to. Nothing had been announced except that she was shot down, and the house wanted to know why.

Jane gave the list of offenses but left out the part about lying on Wayne. She told me that Jeff told her to shut up about it. "It wasn't so much one thing," she said, "as it was a lot of little things."

"So, you let it all build up till you lost your job?" Cathy said.

"What do you care?" Gary asked. "You just want to jump on her now that she's down."

The group felt that, so when Gary said it, they agreed.

"Exactly," Richard Kogut said.

"You're just jealous of her because you've never had a position of authority," Amy Ericson said.

Gary didn't like Cathy, so he let the group turn on her. The next ten minutes were spent going over her latest list of incidents. She was always in trouble so it wasn't hard to do. Jane was relieved until I went after Cathy.

"You're not jealous of Jane's position in the house, Cathy. You're jealous because Wayne Weaver liked her, and hated you," I said. "So, why don't you cop to that?"

"Wayne Weaver didn't hate me."

"He does now…He told me so."

"Why would he hate me?"

"Because you lied on him."

She stopped with her mouth open. "I didn't…"

"Yes, you did," Jane cut her off. "Wayne never had sex with you."

She could see that we were done with the lies, and stared at Jane for a few seconds quietly. Then she began to cry. "It wasn't my fault," she said. "Danny was going to put me in the ring."

"It wasn't anyone's fault," I said. "Yvette, Jane and you have all admitted the same thing." I turned to Willie Garcia. "So let's have it, Willie. You're the one who needs to tell the truth. You're the one they're still torturing him over."

Everyone looked at him. "I say the same thing; Danny was going to hit me."

"So, you made it up?"

"Yeah," he said. "And he hit me anyway."

We talked about false confessions for the rest of the group. The worst of the violence was what the program took from our being. Danny picked the one thing he could take from Wayne that would destroy him, and he did it after he had him beaten. He did that to all of us. When the group was over Gary and I put together the notes and gave them to Jeff Gottlieb, but we never heard about them again.

#

Wayne thanked me, but I could see that nothing would change for him. We played out the season, went 0-8, and I never saw him again. Mike Skakel had a great game against Brunswick the last game of the season, and we walked away feeling respectable. Jamie Newfield led us in a song on the bus ride home.

"We're best friends, we'll always be…Tackles and kicks, and blocks and blitz…Friends, we'll be."

For us, there was justice because we publicly hung Danny Bennison in that group and no one was afraid. We also talked about what he did to Mary Jones. We thumbed our nose at the program for a minute and got away with it. What's more, I pulled it off without losing my job.

Cathy Collins took care of that.

Chapter Fifteen

When Cathy Collins split, she was caught in a few hours because she didn't want to get away. She was dressed in shorts in the cold. Cathy wasn't stupid so if she wanted to escape she would have planned better.

At her general meeting Jeff put her in the ring, spanked her with the paddle and shot her down. He gave her a sign, assigned her a P.O. and gave her a twenty minute lecture. None of it was unexpected. After eighteen months in the program I knew what was going to happen before it did...except for what happened next.

Donna Bouton was Cathy's escort when she ran, so Jeff shot her down and gave her the same sign to wear. Then, he did the same to Gary Ross because he was her boss and me because I was his. I had heard of that happening but had never seen it done. I fell from the top to the bottom that easily. It was the third time I had been shot down and all three times I hadn't done anything wrong. The slogan about injustices was right.

My sign said 'Hi, my name is Wayne Kernochan. Please ask me why I'm too busy trying to impress people to be responsible for the people in my house'. It wasn't very humiliating insofar as signs went and Jeff told me that it would be a short shot-down, so I took it well at first. Things rarely went according to plan in Élan. No one took Joe Peterson into account.

\#

Amy Ericson came to me in the kitchen. "You have to knock on the coordinator's office door."

Joe was the only coordinator in the house and his haircuts were always motivated by anger and degradation. He talked about the military and discipline, but had little to offer in the way of therapy. I prepared for idiocy.

If you hadn't done anything wrong, it was probably a generic haircut with a theme that made no sense. Those could be about your lackadaisical attitude because your bed wasn't made well, or your problem with authority because you weren't cleaning the kitchen floor fast enough. They bored me. Joe didn't.

"Do you know why you're standing there?" he asked.

"No." I stared at him blankly as he screamed at me about trying to impress people. It was boring until it became about my sexuality, and me being gay. "I'm not gay."

Joe stopped. "Get back out, and knock on that door."

I did.

"Who's out there?"

"Wayne."

"Come in!"

I did.

"Do you know why you're standing there?"

"No."

He screwed up his face, and screamed with all his might about me having the audacity to interrupt him while he was giving a haircut and segued into me admitting to being gay in a general meeting, so I interrupted him again.

"I didn't admit to that; ask anyone that was there."

"Get out, and knock on that door again."

I did, and he didn't ask me if I knew why I was standing there. He said it. "I'm not even going to ask you why you're standing there…" and he went on for twenty minutes.

Joe was trying to humiliate me in front of the house with lies and I wasn't going to let him. After knocking on the door for the eighth time, he yelled "Come in!" and when I entered Jeff was standing there.

"What the fuck is your problem?" He didn't want an answer. He cut me off as I was about to. "You don't run this house anymore. Get that through your head."

When he was done, Joe made me knock twice more; once for making Jeff take time out of his schedule for a nobody like me, and the second for wanting to impress people. He left the gay thing alone.

\#

The bathroom was the hardest work for people that were shot down. Joe Peterson was an Army man so he knew that and gave me the dirtiest work—the toilets. After my defiance, he had me scrub them with a toothbrush. I had also heard of that before but never seen it.

"I want this door open all the time," Joe said. "You're not going to run off and get me shot down like Cathy did to you. You know what? I think you'd do it just to get me shot down."

"No, I wouldn't."

"Get out, and knock on that door, Wayne Kerningham."

Joe always mispronounced my name. If I corrected him again it would just be another door to knock on, and another and another. I already told him in an encounter group and he continued doing it, so I got used to it.

When he was done blasting me for talking back, I took the pail of water and the toothbrush and started cleaning the toilet. He left. There was a shortage of people in positions in the house so I was left without a P.O. When Lisa Kelch came by, I asked if I could close the door to use the bathroom and she said I could, so I locked the door, took out the razor blade and cut the bottoms of my feet until they bled.

I bit my hand until it had two semi circular purple imprints of teeth. When the initial pain went away, the euphoria settled in and I exhaled. I wrapped toilet paper around the cuts to soak up the blood, put on my socks and shoes and opened the door

\#

Over the next week I cut myself. Staff only looked at your wrists because the cutters in the house wanted attention. I didn't. I wanted the pain. It made the crazy go away and with Joe Peterson in charge of the house, I needed that.

When Gary and Jane told Joe that I had never admitted to being gay, he changed his assessment of me, and from that point on everything I did wrong was because I didn't feel like a man and was afraid women wouldn't accept me. He obviously wasn't in Denise's group.

There were always a few that would jump on a bandwagon no matter how stupid it was, so Eric States and Matt Brennan started saying that I was feminine, and made fun of me for it. Joe told them to knock it off, but he smirked when he did.

\#

I was cutting when Lisa knocked on the bathroom door.

"Wayne, you need to knock on Jeff's door."

I said "Give me one minute."

"Now."

I grabbed the end of the toilet paper and pulled it too hard, leaving half of the roll on the floor. "I need a minute to get decent."

"Hurry up."

I wrapped my feet and dropped the razor blade into my shoe. Then I pulled on my socks, put my shoes on and wiped the blood from my hands with the extra paper. I flushed, opened the door and went to Jeff's office to knock.

"Who's out there?" Jeff asked.

"Wayne."

"Come in."

His voice was calm so I relaxed and opened the door. There was a chair where I was supposed to stand which was usually an indication that you were going to be spanked, but Jeff didn't have an angry tone in his voice, so it was a talking-to.

A talking-to was a haircut without the yelling. The convoluted therapy was the same so it was useless to me, but at least it wasn't another haircut. It was Jeff, Joe and Jane. I looked at Jeff.

"Do you know why you're in here?"

"No."

"Sit down."

I did.

"Look," Jeff said. "I'm not gonna pull any punches with you. You were my coordinator and I like ya...you're a good guy." He sighed. "But, Jesus Christ man, you're making it hard on me and my crew."

He told me that I wasn't long from going home, but that I wasn't going until I straightened out and did my thing. He finished. "When you go out of this office, I want you to change the way you act, okay?"

I nodded.

Joe was uncomfortable doing a talking-to. He stammered because he was angry, and blamed everything on the fact that I had a bad relationship with my mother. I wanted to correct him because in spite of all the problems at home, I didn't, but Jeff was there so I left it alone.

Jane told me that she had respect for me but was losing it as my behavior got worse. When she was done, Jeff spoke again. "I want to see a marked improvement in you," he said. "Now get out."

I went back to the bathroom, closed the door and cut some more.

#

By lunchtime that day the pain was almost too much to hide. It took more cutting to get the same high so in a short time I needed to stop. I ran out of safe places to hide the evidence. When I needed relief, I hyperventilated but that gave me headaches and didn't last very long. Joe became more vicious, so I got worse still. I left the talking-to with every intention of trying to get my job back, and mutilated myself in the bathroom to try and make it happen, but there was no way I was going to let Joe Peterson win.

It was going to be another long winter.

Chapter Sixteen

I complained about the snow and cold because Joe liked to torture me, so he put me outside. The more I complained, the more opportunities he found to do it. It was a painful cold but it was my favorite place in the world. The P.O. rotated out every hour and none of them paid me much attention, and best of all Joe was too busy to get a turn.

The bitter air had another perk. My hands, face and feet hurt so much that I stopped cutting myself. The harsh winter chill took its place, and I did well outside.

Julie Amundsen was shot down with me. We touched each other in front of Joe. He was convinced that I was gay so he didn't say a word. We were in what Élan called 'a contract' because we flirted with each other.

Jeff game me a promotion to department head of the radio crew a week after I got outside. It was a new department. Maintenance men came and put speakers all through the house. My days with the Shot Pulling Newspaper convinced Jeff to give me the position.

"If you give me two weeks without any incidents, I'll put you on a plane home," he said. "I'm gonna keep you out of meetings and groups, you can do night man four, five days a week." He stood up and shook my hand. "It's time for you to go home,"

\#

Joe Peterson was made full coordinator and Amy Ericson was made my boss, so he had no reason to speak to me. Amy had no responsibility as my boss so she was also made the service crew coordinator. Jeff could see what was going on between Joe and me and wanted us apart.

The radio room was a walk-in closet before it became my office, and though it was small, it had everything I needed to deejay for the house. I sat down, hung up the schedule and was going through the records when Julie came to the door.

"This is the coolest fucking job in this place, dude," she said. "I'm so jealous."

"It is pretty sweet, huh?"

"Sweet?" she said. "This is sex and candy, combined. And I heard you're going home."

"How did you hear about that?"

"I have my sources."

I moved some records and Julie saw the Lynyrd Skynyrd album. She said, "Free bird!" a little too loudly.

"Hey," I said. "Keep it down."

"Yes, Mister Department Head."

"Hey, fuck you. I'm not like that."

"Sorry." She laughed. "So, when are you gonna play our song?"

I played it first.

\#

When I was promoted, Julie stopped acting out and was promoted to department head of the service crew. She had as much time in as I did and was talking about going home as well. The door to my office opened into her new office. When I came out she was standing there waiting for me, dressed up and holding a clipboard.

"You look better in shorts," I said.

"Hey, fuck you."

"I'm complimenting your legs."

"Yeah, well, I ain't getting shot down so you can look at my legs."

"Too bad," I said. "Ya got nice gams."

"Thanks."

\#

I got another candy bar for Christmas that year. We all did. The other thing I got was my first kiss. It was in my office with Julie Amundsen. We broke a cardinal rule on Jesus' birthday, and no one ever found out.

"For it to be guilt, you have to feel guilty, right?" Julie said.

I nodded.

105

"Ya feel guilty?"

"No."

"Then there's nothing to cop to."

I kissed her again.

The world started to make sense again. Through two years of backwards logic and brutal insanity, Julie kept one foot on the ground, and that night she helped me put one down as well. I didn't care that I was going home with a bellyful of guilt. Kissing a girl was the sanest thing I had ever done in the state of Maine.

\#

Gary Ross and Jane Tolar left a few days before me, and my peers were gone. I got in less trouble than any of them and stayed the longest. Like everything else, it didn't make sense. I stayed in my office, avoided people and did night man six days a week, and eventually they sent me home.

It was hollow because everyone was gone. Even most of the peers below me had gone before me. The house congratulated me but the people I survived the worst of it with were gone. I envied the young residents who didn't have to deal with the insanity of directors like Danny and Joe. I liked them, and told them about the old days when the house was corrupt.

Everyone said how much they were going to miss my stories and sense of humor. I stumbled out the front door of Élan like the last drunk at closing time. They put me on a bus in the snow to a train station in New York City, where I would begin my new life.

\#

Four years later, on the day I got out of prison, Roy Sullivan, the park ranger from Virginia, put a gun in his mouth and pulled the trigger. I shook my head and laughed when I heard so the guard asked what I was laughing about. I thought about the day we found out that Matt Brennan jerked off in his sleep.

"We're driving, right?"

Epilogue

On March 23rd, 2011, my forty-eighth birthday, the Lewiston Sun Journal announced that the Élan school was closing. On April 1st, 2011, Élan finally closed its doors, on the twenty-eighth anniversary of the day I burned down my family's home.

Before attending Élan, I had never been arrested, had never done drugs. Two years after I got out of Élan, I was addicted and in prison. I was one of many ex-residents whose lives went awry after their brutal form of therapy. Many didn't make it. On the day it closed, I didn't feel closure. Hopefully others did; their nightmare was over.

Joe Ricci's widow, Sharon Terry, was the owner of Élan. She blamed the closing on internet attacks and a smear campaign launched against the school by a person called Gzasmyhero. I had never heard of him. I knew him as Jeff Wimbleton; Gzasmyhero went by many names.

The Sun Journal in Lewiston, Maine, ran stories along with many powerful statements. A few caught my attention. One best fit my memory of Élan: *"Former student Matt Hoffman, who boarded at Élan between 1974 and 1976, had nothing good to say about the program Wednesday, calling the campus a 'sadistic, brutal, violent, soul-eating hellhole." Lewiston Sun Journal, March 24th, 2011*

I put my book up on the internet for free when someone convinced me that I would never get a publisher. I had just gotten a rejection from my agent on another book, and did it in the heat of the moment. My timing couldn't have been better. On March 31st, this book made the news:

"The tales of treatment at the school during the 1970's were well-documented during the 2002 murder trial of former student Michael Skakel, and the practices of isolating students, screaming sessions called 'general meetings' and physically rough treatment have been written about by dozens of former students, including

disturbing details of Wayne Kernochan's time at the school between 1978 and 1980 detailed in his e-book, 'A Life Gone Awry: My Story of the Élan School'."~The Lewiston Sun Journal

Though there were disagreements about the school voiced on different internet groups prior to April 1st, 2011 some people also planned internet parties and get-togethers. When Élan was finally closed, most of us were quiet. The planned get-togethers never happened. It was a bittersweet victory.

On April 5th, 2011, Clare Woodman, a longtime Élan staff member, confronted Sean Garbleman on a internet site. She claimed she had evidence he was Gzasmyhero, that the authorities had seen his internet service provider for a minute, and that Élan had been watching him for weeks. I told her that I had asked Sean to do it, and that I was Gzasmyhero, and knew they were watching me. She never responded.

"One thing is sure, is that they don't have any idea who it is," I wrote to Jeff Wimbleton. "They would have loved to hang me publicly." He agreed, and said he didn't know if Sean was Gzasmyhero.

The news of Élan's closing drew a lot of internet attention. I was introduced to an online society that had been waging war against Élan for ten years. They introduced me to a world that extended beyond mainstream social media, into blogs, message boards, and chat rooms, and gave me access to a fake profile that was watching everyone. Whoever sent me that profile and password could read everyone's private messages if he wanted. It was fascinating.

There are so many fake profiles on the internet that I still don't know who Jeff Wimbleton was. but I have found at least one person who knew the intimate facts of our relationship. I still don't know if he's who he says he is. I'll be sure when or if we meet. While I'm sure this person is Jeff Wimbleton, I'm not sure Jeff Wimbleton is who he says he is. The internet is confusing.

In the real world, I had told Élan that I was Gzasmyhero, and the Sun Journal named me as a core campaign member in the attempts to get the school closed. I was the guy who wrote the book. Sharon Terry should have sued me, but she was silent. Élan slipped into the past, and the trees in the woods of Poland Springs stopped making noise. For people who didn't want to stare at a tragedy, it was over. My book was buried in a Sun Journal article, twenty paragraphs deep. It went away quietly as well.

Matt Hoffman, Mark Babitz, Felice Eliscu and Sharon McCarthy became my online family. Together, we planned a book and tried to provoke Sharon Terry to sue me so we could tell our stories publicly. When Élan closed, and the planned get-togethers didn't happen, it felt like a hollow victory, but when there was no story in the newspapers on the day Élan closed, it felt like a cover up.

There were remarkably few posts on the book's page, and there wasn't a single inflammatory remark. One poignant message from Matt Hoffman stays with me: *"Wayne's book about Élan, lucid, vivid, captures the grist and grinding of what it was like to be in Élan, even during my time which was 7-74 to 7-76.(a couple of years before Wayne). This book touches me to my very being. It cuts thru to the marrow in my bones."*

One quote from the internet group, Fornits, hit me hardest: *"This story brought up old hurts, wounds and anger. I was a resident at Élan for almost 2 years, I watched Élan change into a violent atmosphere in a matter of years. I witnessed the change in residents being brought to Élan from Mental facilities, Juvenile detention centers, Autistic children ect....I watched Staff and Directors leave en-mass and I watched 3 people who are still there deny they are doing children harm, It is beyond shameful."* ~Danny Bennison

Until Michael Skakel's trial, I thought Élan had closed. This book began when I bought a computer in 2001 and stumbled onto the story. I also had no idea that there were other programs like it until after Élan announced they were closing. I hadn't told anyone what happened to me in Élan. I told people that I had been in prison. The idea that there were other programs like it was too insane to consider, but it happened.

From Synanon, to the Seed, to Straight Inc, the worst parts of the program were adopted across the country as therapy. I fell into a dark depression. The night of my forty eighth birthday, I cut myself for the first time in years. Élan made me bleed some more.

The worst part of Élan's demise was that it went out with a whimper. Only a few papers mentioned it. Outside the internet, very few people heard the story. Élan's legacy is a trail of tears, but the people of the state of Maine want the stain erased. To them, it was over on April 1st, 2011.

The fear and nightmares over the previous thirty years were for nothing. Élan wasn't a monster watching and waiting. I was a number to them. They couldn't be bothered with me after the money ran out.

Danny Bennison and I have worked out a relationship that benefits us and the world around us. We're working together to bring awareness to the troubled teen industry. Danny agreed to let this book go to print to benefit organizations that fight abuse in programs like Élan. They are still practicing, and there are a lot of them. Élan closed down, but it didn't go away. Without a fight, it never will.

APPENDIX 1

RESOURCES AND ASSISTANCE FOR SURVIVORS

International Survivors Action Committee (ISAC)
Specialty Schools and Referral Companies Watch List
Extensive Reference, Research and Database Library

Michelle Sutton Memorial Fund
Buyer Beware: "A Parent's Worst Nightmare" by Catherine Sutton

HEAL Online
Excellent Discussion Forum, Industry-Related Links and Other
Resources for Parents and Alumni of Specialty Schools & Programs.

TROUBLED TEEN INDUSTRY.com

Help At Any Cost
Official website for the critically acclaimed best-seller "Help At Any Cost: How The Troubled Teen Industry Cons Parents and Hurts Kids"

www.cafety.org/

http://wellspringretreat.org/

Bill & Lorna Goldberg: cult recovery counseling
(201) 894-8515

http://www.rickross.com/dvds/dvd.html

http://freedomofmind.com/

Cafety
www.cafety.org -- Community Alliance for the Ethical
Treatment of Youth (CAFETY) is a member-driven advocacy
organization that promotes and secures the human rights of
vulnerable youth confined in residential programs or who are at
risk of being confined in such programs.

Dedication:

Aaron Wright Bacon (16 years old), died 3/31/94 -- untreated Peritonitis

Alex Cullinane (13 years old), died 8/12/06 – under investigation

Alex Harris (12 years old) died 9/13/05 – dehydration and a blow to his head

Andrew McClain (11 years old) died 3/22/98 – traumatic asphyxiation and chest compression

Angellika 'Angie' Arndt (7 years old) died 26/05/06 – traumatic asphyxiation while restrained

Anthony Dumas (15 years old) died 6/12/00 – hanged himself. Home workers did not cut him down, took pictures, police cut him down. He died 4 months later, never coming out of his coma

Anthony Green (15 years old) died 5/21/91 -- Traumatic asphyxiation

Anthony T Haynes (14 years old) died 7/1/2001 – dehydration

Bobby Joe Randolph (17 years old) died 9/26/96 – traumatic asphyxiation

Bobby Sue Thomas (17 years old) died 8/16/96 – acute cardiac arrhythmia while restrained

Brandon Hadden (18 years old) 1998 – choked on his vomit while being restrained

Brendan Blum (14 years old) died 6/28/07 – bowel obstruction

Bryan Dale Alexander (18 years old) -- pneumonia

Caleb Jensen (15 years old) died 5/2007 – untreated severe staph infection

Cameron Hamilton (2 years old) died 12/5/05 -- severe head trauma

Candace Newmaker (10 years old) 4/18/2000 – death resulting from rebirthing

Carlton Eugene Thomas (17 years old) – restraint

Casey Collier (17 years old) 12/93 – traumatic asphyxiation

Cedric Napoleon (14 years old) 3/7/2002 – restraint

Chad Andrew Franza (16 years old) 8/17/98 – suicide by hanging

Charles "Chase" Moody Jr (17 years old) 10/14/02 – asphyxiation by restraint

Charles Collins Jr (15 years old) – forced over-exercise with known heart condition

Chloe Cohen died 2/21/? – suicide by hanging

Christopher Michael (8 years old) died 11/24/02 – abuse

Chris Campbell (13 years old) died 11/2/97 – undetermined.

Christie Scheck (13 years old) died 3/6/92 – suicide by hanging

Cindi Sohappy (16 years old) died 12/6/03 – undetermined

Corey William Murphy (17 years old) died 3/21/2000 – suicide

Daniel Matthews (17 years old) died 3/31/03 – killed by fellow inmate

Danieal Kelly (14 years old) died 8/4/06 – starvation, dehydration, cerebral palsy

Darryl Thompson (15 years old) died 10/06 – restraint

Dawn Renay Perry (16 years old) died 4/10/93 – restraint death

Dawnne Takeuchi (18 years old) died 6/25/95 – thrown from moving vehicle

Diane Harris (17 years old) died 4/11/90 – violently restrained, asphyxiation

Dillon Taylor Peak (14 years old) died 6/17/06 – severe untreated encephalitis

Donderey Rogers died July 2002 – restraint

Dustin E Phelps (14 years old) died 3/1/98 – strapped in a blanket in bed

Earl Smith (9 years old) died 1/11/95 – asphyxiation while restrained

Edith Campos (15 years old) died 2/2/98 – restraint asphyxiation

Elisa Santry (16 years old) died 7/16/2006 – under investigation

Eddie Lee (15 years old) -- restrained, beaten

Eric Roberts (16 years old) died 2/22/96 – wrapped in plastic foam blanket

Erica Harvey (15 years old) died 5/27/2002 – hypothermia and dehydration

Faith Finley (17 years old) died 12/31/2006 – suffocated while being restrained

Gareth Myatt (15 years old) died 4/04 – restraint

Garrett Halsey (16 years old) died 12/23/04 – autistic and mentally retarded, restraint death

Gina Score (14 years old) died 1990 – hyperthermia

Ian August (14 years old) died 7/13/2002 – hyperthermia

Isaiah Simmons died 1/23/2007 – restrained

Jamal Odum (9 years old) – restraint death

Jamar Griffiths (15 years old) died 10/18/94 – traumatic asphyxiation

James White (17 years old) died 12/05

Jamie Young (13 years old) died 6/5/93 – heatstroke and dehydration with overdose of antidepressants

Jason Tallman (12 years old) died 5/12/93 – suffocated while restrained

Jeffrey Bogrett (9 years old) died 12/1/95 – restraint

Jeffry Demetrius (17 years old) died 9/26/97 – strangulation while being restrained

Jerry Mclaurin (14 years old) died 11/2/99 – restraint

Jimmy Kanda (6 years old) died 9/20/97-- strangulation while restrained in wheelchair

Joey (Giovanni) Alteriz (16 years old) died 2/4/06 – asphyxiation while restrained

John McCloskey (18 years old) died 2/24/96 – ruptured colon, torn liver, torn small intestine from being sodomized with a broom-like handle

Johnny Lim (14 years old) died 12/26/05 spontaneous brain-stem hemorrhage

Jonathan Carey (13 years old) died 2/15/07 – asphyxiation while restrained in van

Joshua Ferarini (13 years old) died 1/8/89 – suffocation while restrained

Joshua Sharpe (17 years old) died 12/28/99 – restraint

Karlye Newman (16 years old) died 10/8/2004 – suicide by hanging

Kasey Warner (13 years old) died 10/8/2005 – drowning
Katherine Lank (16 years old) died 1/13/2002 – massive head trauma
Katherine Rice (16 years old) died 5/2/2008 – overdose of methadone
Kelly Young (17 years old) died 3/4/98 – position asphyxiation while restrained
Keyana Bravo-Hamilton (2 years old) died 9/4/06 – abuse, internal injuries
Kerry Layne Brown (24 years old) died 6/6/06 –
Kristal Mayon-Ceniceros (16 years old) died 2/5/99 – respiratory arrest from restraint
Kristen Chase (16 years old) died 6/27/90 – heatstroke
Kyle Young (16 years old) – pushed by guards into elevator doors that opened, he fell down the shaft
LaKeisha Brown (17 years old) died 4/9/2005 – medical neglect
Latasha Bush (15 years old) died 2/14/2002 – restraint asphyxiation
Lenny Ortega (12 years old) died 5/31/2002 – drowned
Linda Harris (14 years old) died 9/18/2005 – asphyxiation while restrained
Leroy Prinkley (14 years old) died 9/28/88 cerebral anoxia from forceful restraint
Maria Mendoza (14 years old) died 10/12/2003 – traumatic asphyxiation while restrained
Marcus Fiesel (3 years old) died Aug 2006 – taped into high chair, left for two days, then his body burned. Cause of death unknown
Mario Cano (16 years old) – blood clot
Mark Draheim (14 years old) died 12/98 – asphyxiation while restrained
Matthew Goodman (14years old) died 2/6/2002 – pneumonia, respiratory distress and blood poisoning from being kept in mechanical restraints for 16 months
Mark Soares (16 years old) died 4/29/98 cardiac arrest from physical restraint
Martin Lee Anderson (14 years old) died 1/6/2006 – asphyxiation from ammonia capsules being shoved up his nose

A Life Gone Awry: My Story of the Elan School

Melissa Neyman (19 years old) died 7/24/97 – hanged in restraint straps

Michael Arnold (19 years old) died 7/15/97 asphyxiation while restrained

Michael (Christening) Carcia (12 years old) died 12/2005 – restraint

Michael IbarraWiltsie (12 years old) died 2/5/2000 -- asphyxiation while restrained

Michael Lewis III, (15 years old) died 8/25/2003 – restraint

Natalynndria Lucy Slim (16 years old) died 7/13/06) -- suicide by hanging

Nicholas Contreras (16 years old) died 3//98 – prolonged serious medical neglect

Omar Paisley (17 years old) died 6/9/2003 – untreated ruptured appendix

Omega Leach (17 years old) died June 2007 – restraint

Orlena Parker (15 years old) died 3/10/2003 – restraint

Paul Choy (16 years old) died 1992 – restraint

Raijon Daniels (8 years old) died 10/26/06 – prolonged intense abuse

Randy Steele (9 years old) died 2/6/2000 – suffocation while restrained

Robert Doyle Erwin (15 years old) – drowning

Robert Rollins (12 years old) died 4/21/97 – asphyxiation while restrained

Roberto Reyes (15 years old) died 11/3/04 – rhabdomyolysis

Rochelle Clayborne (16 years old) died 8/18/97 – cardiac arrhythmia after receiving tranquilizers

Roxanna Gray (17 years old) died 7/6/89 – suffocation while restrained

Ryan Lewis (14 years old) died 2/13/2001 – suicide by hanging

Sabrina E Day (15 years old) died 2/10/2000 – restraint

Sakena Dorsey (18 years old) died 6/10/97 – suffocation while restrained, history of asthma

Sarah Crider (14 years old) died 2/13/06 – intestinal blockage, bacterial sepsis, vomit in her lungs, infection of the bloodstream

Sergey Blashchishena (16 years old) died 8/28/2009 – cause of death unknown

Shinaul McGraw (12 years old) died 6/5/97 – hyperthermia, wrapped in sheet and restrained with gauze over his mouth

Shawn Smith (13 years old) died 10/30/2001 – suicide by hanging

Shirley Arciszewski (12 years old) died 09/05 -- restraint death, asphyxia

Stephanie Duffield (16 years old) died 2/11/01 – restraint

Stephen Komminos (22 years old) died 10/04/07 – choking

Timothy Thomas (9 years old) – restraint death

Tanner Wilson (11 years old) died 2/9/01 – heart attack while restrained

Anthony 'Tony' Haynes (14 years old) -- Heat exhaustion, suspected abuse

Thomas Mapes (17 years old) died 7/8/94 – asphyxiation while handcuffed

Travis Parker (13 years old) died 4/21/05 – denied asthma medication while restrained

Tristan Sovern (16 years old) died 3/4/98 – asphyxiation while restrained

Unnamed (16 years old) died 7/2/2004 – suicide by hanging

Unidentified (16 years old) died April 2007 – suicide by hanging

Valerie Ann Heron (17 years old) died 8/10/2001 – suicide by jumping from balcony

Victoria Petersilka died 2/9/02 – suicide by hanging

Walter Brown (18 years old) died Jan 2005 – restrained

Wauketta Wallace (12 years old) died 7/11/89 – postural asphyxiation from restraint

Will Futrelle (15 years old) died 3/25/96 – murdered by other students

William (Eddie) Lee (15 years old) died 9/18/2000 – injury at base of skull from being restrained

Willie Lawrence Durden III (17years old) died 10/14/2003 – untreated ventricular arrhythmia

Willie Wright (9 years old) died 2/4/2000 – restraint

Bernard Reefer died 11/24/80

Carlos Ruiz (13 years old) died 12/16/94

Carter Lynn died 6/7/06 – suicide by hanging

Carles Lucas (16 years old) died 11/24/80 – drowning

Christopher Brown (16 years old) died 3/26/03 – hit by train while running away

Corey Baines (16 years old) died 3/26/03 – tree fell on tent while sleeping

Danny Lewis (16 years old) died 6/89

Eric David Schibley (17 years old) died 11/24/80 – drowning

James Lamb (14 years old) died 11/24/80 – drowning

John Avila died 7/25/94

John Vincent Garrison (18 years old)

Kristen Chase (16 years old) died 6/27/90

Laura Hanson (17 years old) died 11/19/98

Leon Anger died 9/16/84

Lorenzo Johnson (17 years old) died 6/27/94 – drowned while running away

Lyle Foodroy – drowned

ML – shot and killed himself

Matt Toppi (17 years old) died 3/7/98 -- hit by train while running away

RC died 4/10/05 -- suicide

Robert Zimmerman (17 years old) died 11/24/80 – drowning

Rocco Magliozzi (12 years old) died 7/28/06 – West Nile Virus and Rocky Mountain Spotted Fever

Tammy Edmiston died 9/11/82

All these children died while in care or as a result of care in residential treatment facilities, boot camps, wilderness programs, behavior modification programs, and other private and state sponsored facilities.

Made in the USA
Middletown, DE
09 April 2021